Praise for
Making a Difference

"Amy Irvine's book is inspirational reading for the average 'green' citizen—an extremely valuable antidote to the nagging, often crippling suspicion that meaningful environmental action proceeds only from Big Government, Big Money or Big Institutions. This book is about Little People ultimately making Big Differences."

—Pete Bodo, Outdoors columnist, *The New York Times*

"*Making a Difference* provides ample evidence that ordinary citizens can make an extraordinary difference. Amy Irvine's inspiring real-life tales of cooperation between grassroots volunteers and enlightened outdoors companies show that there are sensible solutions to our environmental challenges."

—Sal Ruibal, Outdoors writer, *USA Today*

"To anyone who has ever thought one person can't change the world, I say read *Making a Difference*. This powerful book chronicles the sacrifices made by individuals who put everything on the line to fight for the preservation of America's wild places. Not only is it a loving tribute to the efforts of these brave outdoor enthusiasts and the organizations that helped to champion their causes, its infectious, lead-by-example message is a call to action many readers won't ignore. Engaging and

inspirational, *Making a Difference* is a celebration of the fascinating personalities and compelling stories behind grassroots environmental groups and a must-read for anyone who believes a conviction of the heart can move mountains."

—Kelly Pyrek, Editor in Chief, *Outfitter* magazine

"Anyone concerned about the fate of our wildland and wildlife heritage will be cheered by Amy Irvine's lively accounts of the achievements of citizen activists aided by an unusual coalition of outdoors-oriented business enterprises willing to put part of their profits back into conserving that heritage. More power to them!"

—James G. Deane, Editor, *DEFENDERS Magazine*, Defenders of Wildlife

"Read this book. A surge of optimism will surely ignite your passion to stand up for your rights as a citizen of the planet, as this book's heroes have. The stories are living proof that simply doing the right thing, with conviction, can make a big difference in even our own materialist world."

—Amy Schrier, Founder/Editor in Chief, *blue Magazine*

The Conservation Alliance is a group of outdoor businesses whose collective contributions support grassroots citizen-action groups and their efforts to protect wild and natural areas where outdoor enthusiasts recreate. Alliance funds have played a pivotal role in the protection of rivers, trails, wild lands, and climbing areas for muscle-powered recreation.

The Conservation Alliance
Outdoor business giving back to the outdoors.

www.conservationalliance.com

Making a Difference

Stories of
How Our Outdoor Industry and Individuals are
Working to Preserve America's Natural Places

by

AMY IRVINE

FALCON®

Guilford, Connecticut
An imprint of The Globe Pequot Press

Falcon is a registered trademark of The Globe Pequot Press.

Cover and text design by Libby Kingsbury
Cover photo of the Mount Hood Wilderness, Oregon, by Charlie Borland/
    Adventure Photo & Film
Maps by M. A. Dubé

Photo credits: p. 10: Wendy Wilson, Idaho Rivers United; pp. 22, 27, 32: The
Nature Conservancy of Utah; p. 43: Pat O'Hara; p. 50: Ric Careless; p. 55: Ihor
Macijiwsky; p. 65: © Hardie Truesdale; pp. 72, 74: Greg Koop Photography; p.
85: InterTribal Sinkyone Wilderness Council; pp. 96, 103: © Bob Lickter; p. 110:
Doug Perrine; p. 122: Sea Turtle Restoration Project; p. 131: Terrence Moore,
Beartooth Alliance; p. 137: Jim Peaco, Beartooth Alliance; p. 142: Heidi Barrett,
Beartooth Alliance; pp. 152, 158: Charles Little, Tuolumne River Preservation
Trust; p. 172: George Wuerthner; p. 183: Jym St. Pierre; pp. 196, 202: © Doug
Riley-Thron; p. 214: Mark Alan Wilson/picturetomorrow.org; p. 265: Nicholas
Sokoloff

Pemissions are gratefully acknowledged, and listed on page 267.

Library of Congress Cataloging-in-Publication Data

Irvine, Amy.
    Making a difference: stories of how our outdoor industry and
    individuals are working to preserve America's natural places / by
    Amy Irvine.—1st ed.
        p. cm.
    Includes bibliographical references and index.
    ISBN 0-7627-0913-8
    1. Environmentalism—United States. 2. Environmental protection—United
States. 3. Outdoor Industry Conservation Alliance. I. Title.

GE180.I78 2001
333.7'16'0973—dc21

                                                        00-067679

Manufactured in the United States of America
First Edition/Second Printing

For the intrepid staff of the Southern Utah Wilderness Alliance,
they are mentors and family.

And for Herb, my marrow.

A.I.

Contents

Preface

Each of the stories told on these pages could have been a book itself. Compressed into short chapters, the tales may not completely capture just how enduring, complex, and utterly arduous these grassroots conservation efforts were. More important, it was nearly impossible for me to portray in limited space the number of ordinary people who did extraordinary things to save the places they love. In many stories there was more than one Goliath, and in every case there were tens—if not hundreds or thousands—of Davids. I chose to highlight a few of the Davids in each story—to the dismay of each. Every individual you'll read about was adamant that he or she not be singled out; each knew too well that the potency of grassroots activism is forged not from one hero, but from a collective of citizens working in unison.

Know, then, that for each person you'll meet in these pages, there are dozens more just as dedicated. My only regret in telling these tales is that I could not name them all, give them the recognition and honor they each deserve. To all the citizens who threw themselves into these causes, who complicated—and sadly sometimes even lost—their lives for the sake of rivers, forests, mountains, and deserts, I am humbled and in awe.

Amy Irvine

Introduction

This is a book about grassroots environmental organizations —most of them staffed with local volunteers—fighting to save their wild backyards. It's a collection of stories about people who were aghast when they learned that some company or some agency was threatening to cut *their* forests, dam *their* rivers, mine *their* mountains, or develop *their* open meadows. In some cases this initial shock turned to anger, which was then channeled into action; in other cases people's initial doubts about whether they could do anything evolved into a conviction that they had to do something. Best of all, these are stories about people who stood up for what was right, and won.

Behind all these stories is an environmental organization called the Outdoor Industry Conservation Alliance (OICA). This group of companies in the outdoor industry has banded together to give back to the outdoors. Each year, every company in the Alliance gives $1,000 per $1,000,000 of its yearly revenue, with a cap of $10,000, to a fund distributed to small grassroots groups, including those profiled in this book. The member companies also contribute staff to run the Alliance so that 100 percent of the money in the fund is distributed to environmental groups. There is zero overhead.

The Conservation Alliance is a business version of the Christian concept of tithing. Cynics might say that it's in the interest of the companies that are in the Alliance to save the environment, because they depend on the outdoors to make their money. But those of us in the Alliance know the real reason: Our companies are made up of people who cherish the outdoors, who want to use their businesses as vehicles to save wildlands and wildlife, who know that wildness nourishes our souls and energizes our spirits.

Those of us in the OICA also recognize that in many of the stories you will read in this book, our contribution and support were pivotal. They separated victory from defeat. In business—as in all areas of life—there is nothing better than knowing that your effort made a difference. And making a difference is why the Alliance was formed.

The organization was conceived in 1989 after Wally Smith, then CEO of the REI Co-op, read an article by Bill Simon, then CEO of The North Face, lamenting that companies in the outdoor industry weren't doing more to save the outdoors. Wally called Bill and suggested that perhaps they could do something, especially if the companies formed an alliance. Wally then called Yvon Chouinard, who owned Patagonia, and George Grabner of Kelty. All four agreed to contribute $10,000 apiece and award the money to a small group of local activists who were fighting to save the Payette River in Idaho from a series of dams that would drown some of the best white-water runs in North America.

At the next trade show for the outdoor industry, Wally, Bill, George, and Yvon cajoled the heads of dozens more companies to show up for a meeting. Nearly 200 people attended. They clapped loudly when Wally told them they had to band together to save the country's wildlands, when Bill noted that our strength was in our numbers, when George declared it was the right thing to do, and even when Yvon said if they didn't become part of the solution, they were part of the problem.

Then the clapping suddenly quieted when Wally said he wanted each and every director, president, and CEO in the room to pony up ten grand. As the silence continued, some began to steal glances at their neighbors while others stared at their shoes. Then Ron Nadeau stood and introduced himself as the owner of a small company called Grabber that made hand warmers for skiers and outdoorspeople. He told how he had grown up in the Sacramento River delta, lying in bed at night listening to the symphony of the big bullfrogs in the marshlands. He built a cabin on an island in the river, he later brought his new wife there, and he delivered their firstborn there, cutting the cord with his Buck knife. Then one morning he woke to see the beaches covered with black sludge discharging from a Crown Zellerbach factory upriver. The delta became more and more polluted. He abandoned the cabin, and by then the bullfrogs were becoming silent.

The meeting room was also silent. Ron said that his company was tiny; for them $10,000 was an astronomical sum. "But count me in," he added. There was thunderous applause, and another president stood and yelled above the clapping that he was in, too. Then another stood, then another and another. "This feels more like a southern revival than an industry meeting," one said, "and I might wake up tomorrow wondering what in the hell I'm doing, but I'm in for ten grand, too."

More than ten years later we now have about seventy companies in the Conservation Alliance. We loosened the rules so small companies like Ron Nadeau's can get in for a $1,000 contribution, and reps and small retail stores can join for $500. But all still contribute according to the formula of $1,000 per $1,000,000 of revenue, what Yvon Chouinard calls our Earth Tax. Inspired by our example, there is now a very active alliance of outdoor companies in Australia, and another in Japan. Each year we award grants that average between $25,000 and $35,000 to about ten groups; our goal is to increase that figure tenfold or more.

So to any of you reading this who work for companies in the outdoor industry that are not yet members: If we don't hear from you, you can expect to hear from us. We'll be telling you how you *can* make a difference. And if you don't work in the outdoor industry but simply love the outdoors, and you see that some part of *your* sanctuary is being threatened, know that you, too, can make a difference.

If you have any doubts, just read these stories. And know, before you start, that the small grassroots group in Idaho that won our first grant also won its fight. The Payette River is still wild and free.

Rick Ridgeway
President, the Outdoor Industry Conservation Alliance

For more information on the Conservation Alliance, see
www.conservationalliance.com

Making a
Difference

Wed to a River

In 1987, when Wendy Wilson said her wedding vows on the Payette River, it was a typical Idaho day—the kind where the sky gathers everything up into its wide gray skirts and the rain comes in steel-blue sheets. Cold spring air danced off the river and into the little pioneer church that overlooked the water. There Wendy and her beloved bound their lives together before taking the wedding party in a boat down the river to the hot springs.

Fortunately, Wendy had borrowed thirty-five wet suits to keep everyone dry. At the hot springs friends and family gathered under an enormous tent and crowded the picnic tables with potluck delights. There were morel mushrooms. And there was a four-level wedding cake; on its top was a cascading blue river, a canoe, and a bride and groom holding paddles. It was a day perfectly made for lifetime promises.

But Wendy was a wild woman. Just one year later she would make a second set of vows on those same waters.

The Payette had come to mean everything to Wendy. She and her husband, Phil, kayaked and canoed its North, Middle, and South Forks, and it remained the center around which both their lives and their community revolved. A year into their marriage, as the newlyweds digested coffee and the *Idaho Statesman* at the breakfast table, an unimaginable headline caught Wendy's eye.

Boise's infamous billionaire, J. R. Simplot, was planning to drain the North Fork of her river for hydropower. Wendy remembers the man who owned half of Idaho talking to the press

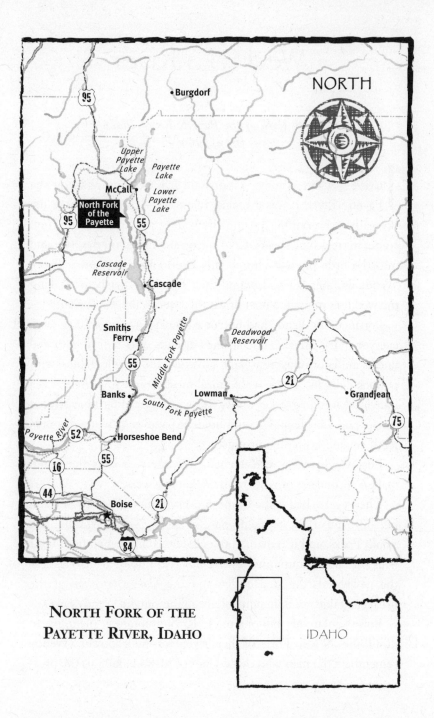

NORTH

Burgdorf

US 95

Upper
Payette
Lake

Payette
Lake

McCall

Lower
Payette
Lake

95

North Fork
of the
Payette

55

Cascade
Reservoir

Cascade

Deadwood
Reservoir

Smiths
Ferry

55

Middle Fork Payette

21

Banks

Lowman

Grandjean

South Fork Payette

75

Payette River

52

Horseshoe Bend

16

55

44

Boise

21

84

IDAHO

NORTH FORK OF THE
PAYETTE RIVER, IDAHO

as if his money could take care of any ecological issues that might stand in his way.

"J. R.'s quote in the paper was so swaggering and arrogant," she recalls. "And that's what got me going."

If J. R. sounds like the vainglorious villain from the 1980s soap *Dallas*, that's because he is rumored to have been the real-life role model for the character. And even if all that the two men share is a first name, wealth, and hubris, that's enough to call them twins. Except TV's J. R. never tried to wrangle a lovely, lively river; the real-life J. R. did.

Not that the Payette is exactly wild. Cows and farms begin to line its banks soon after its headwaters leave the Sawtooth Wilderness of central Idaho. The North Fork is girdled on one side by an Idaho Northern Railroad track, while Highway 55 paves the other. And the days when its waters glittered with thick constellations of sockeye salmon are long gone. Still, the Payette remains one of the great rivers of Idaho, world famous for its trout fishing and boating. It ties the central Idaho wilderness to the Snake River system west of Boise—a lifeline for countless mammals, birds, and fish. And it weaves the sagebrush and sand of the Great Basin desert together with the tall pines and wildflowers of the northern Rockies. It is a quintessentially western landscape, at once lush and spare.

The North Fork is what Wendy fell hardest for. Through the ages its spry, bottle-green waters had charged the valley's granite uplifts, carving out a dramatic gorge ten times steeper than the Grand Canyon. The rapids were some of the most thrilling and challenging anywhere, and their history was an exciting one: In the early 1900s, before the road and railway, loggers actually transported their cut trees down the canyon by riding them like bucking broncos through the North Fork's roughest white water—an exercise that often ended in death by drowning. Since then some great kayakers had lost their lives on the North Fork, too. Indeed, the North Fork was a river to be taken seriously all the way around.

But was the present-day river, in its not-so-pristine state, worth trying to save? Was it worth taking on J. R., one of the hundred richest people in America?

There was no doubt about it in Wendy Wilson's mind. "It's what I call a great backyard river," she says. "It flows through the lives of so many folks and so many communities. It crashes out of the wilderness like a green freight train headed for the sea. It hoots and hollers and swoops you up like you were riding an elk. There are wolves and black bears that still roam its banks. It is home to osprey and trout."

But J. R. didn't seem to care about any of that. Not the bears. Not the boaters. Not even the backyards of his Idaho neighbors. It was a chance to make money—as if the multibillionaire needed any more. The founder of a potato empire that supplies McDonald's with more than half its french fries, this eighth-grade dropout had gone on to bankroll Micron, the famous Boise microchip corporation. After nursing the company through years of ups and downs, J. R.'s share in Micron mushroomed from $2.5 billion to $3.4 billion in just two years—which meant he was harvesting $5 million per workday. Now J. R. was poised to cash in on the Payette, too—by diverting its flow to an underground power generating plant whose electricity would be sold to California's big cities.

A Second Vow

A few days later Wendy Wilson sat in her kayak in an eddy on the North Fork. She was in line to surf Cocaine, a popular wave on the Cabarton stretch. She was disgusted with J. R.'s plan and said so to John Watts in the boat next to her. The Idaho Power Company (IPC) had already dropped the project in 1986 because it couldn't justify the $218 million price tag when there was an energy surplus throughout the state. So J. R. had picked up where the IPC left off. His plan was to dam the North Fork just above the spot where Wendy and John sat, then flood Round Valley, a long, lark-laden meadow cradled by the rocky peaks of the Boise National Forest. "There ought to be a law against somebody just coming in and developing a public resource for private gain," Wendy grumbled.

Wendy was complaining to the right guy. John Watts was a political organizer who told his kayaking companion to quit whining. "If you were a real environmentalist, you'd form a group and stop this thing," he said.

Then and there Wendy committed herself to the river. It was a moment that changed her life.

With John's help she pulled it together in a single evening at an Idaho Whitewater Association meeting. Wendy stood up in front of the Boise boaters to describe the possible fate of the Payette's most formidable fork. Then she asked who was on board with her. From a quiet corner of the room, a kayaker who worked as an engineer for Hewlett-Packard (HP) raised his hand.

Scott Montgomery was a middle-of-the-road guy originally from Minnesota, not the liberal activist that Wendy was. He had only come to the meeting because a colleague at HP had asked him to; the coworker figured Scott would make a good representative for HP boaters, since Scott had recently reassembled the employee ski club. Such a deed made Scott a do-gooder—though Scott wasn't sure that qualified him as a grassroots activist.

But Scott *was* a boater and he loved the Payette dearly—especially the rambunctious rapids of the North Fork. "I used to head to the river every night after work," he says. "I'd take my kayak, a book, and whatever I could find in the fridge for dinner. I'd paddle till I was starved then sit on the shore and eat and read until dark. That was my life for years."

When he gave Wendy his name, his plan had been to spend a few weeks helping the infant group raise some funds—just to help it get going. After all, his engineering job at Hewlett-Packard was a demanding one. And he needed his time on the river. But Scott took his short-term commitment seriously, and soon he had all kinds of HP employees contributing their services and talents—a stark contrast to what Micron's benefactor was doing on the other side of the fence. Scott began his recruitment after a lunchtime meditation session, asking someone from the graphic design department to craft a logo for the group. Others then donated silk-screened T-shirts, golf shirts, and hand-thrown coffee mugs with the new logo emblazoned across. Scott delivered the goods to Wendy. Soon they were selling, and a small stream of money began to flow for Friends of the Payette (FOP). Scott was pleased with his efforts and, having done his part, looked forward to having his weekends and evenings free again.

But Friends of the Payette needed to get serious. They scheduled a meeting at the Boise Public Library, but Wendy Wilson couldn't speak publicly, even as the volunteer leader of FOP. Her "real" employer—that is, the one that cut her paychecks—had made it clear that her extracurricular activities were in conflict with the organization. So Wendy asked Scott if he'd be willing to make the presentation.

Scott had never spoken publicly in his life. He was a quiet guy who split his time between a desk and a boat. And the gathering was daunting; when he arrived at the library, the place was elbow to elbow with people. The press was there, too.

In his even-handed, methodical way, Scott told the community about Friends of the Payette and its plans to organize against the North Fork project. He didn't come at it as an ecofreak ready to chain himself to a dam. Instead he blew apart the project's engineering, explaining each of the flaws in its design. He finished by demonstrating how existing dams along the Payette were poorly run and only operating at 50 percent efficiency. Why not maximize those dams' production rather than putting in yet another project that would greatly affect everyone's enjoyment of the river?

That night there was a union between most unusual partners. Scott couldn't believe the response—not just from environmentalists but also from anglers, private property owners with homes along the North Fork, rafting companies, even jet skiers and ranchers. Many of these folks wouldn't normally be caught dead in a room full of longhairs. But as Scott puts it, "Even though the landowners didn't necessarily like looking down at the river and seeing the naked butts of the kayaking crowd, they knew we had to unite to save the river." By the end of the evening, all the FOP T-shirts and mugs had been sold and the money was on its way to the bank.

Wendy appointed Scott her new codirector. The passionate, bleeding-heart environmentalist and the cool-headed engineer were a match made in heaven.

The two directors could see the necessity of bringing diverse groups together to fight the project and were thrilled that such a wide range of folks was declaring fidelity to the group. But Wendy knew they needed prominent business leaders, too, so with trepidation she scheduled a meeting with the Boise Chamber of Commerce. She recalls that night: "When I first drove up to the Boise County Courthouse, the building was pitch black. Maybe no one was there, I thought. Maybe I'd be lucky to get out alive. What if the lumber mill workers and cattlemen didn't like city girls with an attitude? What if they all secretly wanted to be construction workers and switch-flippers for a power company?"

Wendy eventually found the chamber members waiting for her in the back room. And to her surprise, she was cordially received by most of the group; many grasped that the quality of life in Boise and the surrounding towns depended upon a healthy, free-flowing river. More than a dozen chamber businesses endorsed Friends of the Payette that evening—which gave the group the clout it would need when it went up against the conservative Idaho Legislature. Plus, the group would begin to be viewed as moderate in a state that despised radicals. "The chamber helped soften our image," Wendy says.

But not all businesses were on board—even if they supported the cause, some were afraid of the controversy. Despite her willingness to duck the press, Wendy's employer eventually told her to choose between her job and the river; her politics and outspokenness were in conflict with the organization.

In a reaffirmation of what was most important in life, Wendy chose the river.

For months Wendy, Scott, the steering committee, and many volunteers worked without any pay; the little money that was coming in was directed immediately toward photocopies and phone bills. But Wendy didn't care about the cash. This fight had come to represent all she stood for. "I chose to live in Idaho because I love wild water and wild places. I had run away from the rivers of the Midwest—which were polluted, dammed to perdition, and full of fish I couldn't eat if I wanted to have babies. I felt that if our nation was going to let the Payette go down the tubes literally to line a rich man's pocket, then there was no place left for me to run. I couldn't move any farther 'out West' to get away from this mentality. I was going to have to stand and fight. If we hadn't won . . . well, we just had to win."

Making Headway

Three months after Scott made the first presentation, Wendy and the others stood before the Idaho Water Resources Board with a petition containing more than nine thousand signatures. The petition asked the board to place the river under "interim" protected status until further studies and a management plan could be completed. Under 1986 federal amendments to the Federal Power Act, states could prepare and submit such plans—which in many cases could halt hydropower projects that would otherwise be approved by the feds. No other state in the nation had developed such a plan. Amazingly, the board agreed to do so—after all, it was a great way to address the argument of FOP's opponents that they were locking up the river forever.

In the meantime, it appeared that J. R. was exasperated with the public protest Friends of the Payette had created, and the project was no longer worth his time. The Micron man washed his hands of the deal and transferred his company's water rights to Gem Irrigation District, a down-and-out water diversion company that was looking for a speculative scheme to generate some cash flow.

In 1989 Gem proposed an alternative design for the project on the North Fork, since the original had been so heavily hacked by Friends of the Payette. This one was no better: It still intended to divert the North Fork's water, but the flooding would occur in High Valley, a quiet ranching community interspersed with summer homes. Gem was certain it could slide the project through; ultimately, it didn't matter if the proposal was a bad one—image was everything, and the local irrigation company came across as a downtrodden farmer. The public's heart would go out to Gem far more than it had to J. R.

But Friends of the Payette didn't care about image. It sent volunteers into High Valley to knock on each door and educate the townspeople on the dam that would damn their property. From every resident the reaction was the same: They were furious, because Gem had never even contacted them about the project— let alone mentioned that they were planning on condemning the residents' properties for it. All of High Valley pledged its support to Friends of the Payette.

Finding the Funds to Win

Although the river now had some temporary protection, the real showdown would take place in the chambers of the Idaho State Legislature, where the water board's plan would be accepted or rejected. It was time to go after serious money to fund Friends' lobbying efforts. Wendy kicked into fund-raising mode and began to research possible sources to fit the bill. The problem was, most foundations were uncomfortable funding aggressive lobbying activity, because it put them under the scrutiny of the IRS. And many individual folks had a difficult time donating to lobbying work, because it wasn't tax deductible. As FOP members watched

A canoeist rides the popular Cabarton stretch of the Payette's North Fork.

their bank-account numbers drop into the single digits, it looked as though the honeymoon might be over.

It was REI's Kathleen Beamer who saved the day. She first told Wendy about the Outdoor Industry Conservation Alliance (OICA) when Wendy called her to get some direction on funding sources. Kathleen explained that the Alliance, then in its early stages of courtship with outdoor industry businesses, was forming with the intention of supporting environmental groups' aggressive political activity when necessary. At that point Wendy had nothing to lose. She approached Patagonia and Perception Kayaks, two Alliance members, to sponsor a proposal from Friends of the Payette. They responded that she couldn't write the proposal fast enough.

Wendy cranked out a proposal over Thanksgiving weekend, while the rest of the nation sat down to say grace over a table full of food. She sent it off with her own prayer attached.

The Conservation Alliance's First Grant

The Conservation Alliance responded by inviting Scott to come speak at its first-ever funding meeting in Las Vegas. "It was such a cool atmosphere," he recalls. "Here were all these hard-core outdoor recreationists turned entrepreneurs, sitting around talking about saving wild places. I remember Yvon Chouinard, the climbing legend and founder of Patagonia, pushing the group to help with wolf restoration. He was joking about naming each wolf in the pack after a Conservation Alliance member company: Gore-Tex, REI, Patagonia . . . you get the picture. It was really a wonderful day."

After his presentation, Scott panicked. He was afraid he'd offended the executives—most of whom were California residents. "There I was, rattling on about our Idaho rivers being used to fire up hot tubs in their state; boy, was I embarrassed. I thought, 'Well, there goes our shot at funding.'"

But the Alliance folks didn't care one bit about Scott's cutting remarks—they knew he was right and respected him for his straight shooting. When Scott sat down a representative from Gore, the maker of Gore-Tex fabric, rose and spoke fervently. "Where I'm from, we get a lot of emotion and inspiration when we're gathered together in church. But I've got that same feeling here—like I'm part of something much larger. I am so inspired. There's no way my company wouldn't help with this."

Following that speech the Conservation Alliance made its first grant ever—$40,000 to Friends of the Payette. "It was the most money I'd ever seen in one place," says Wendy.

The chunk of change spurred intense activity. Scott began traveling statewide, forming partnerships with unusual groups that all supported the protection of the North Fork. His time on the river had been replaced with time at citizens' meetings, making presentations about Gem's flawed project design. His bosses at Hewlett-Packard began to ask if he actually still worked for them;

he seemed to be seen only on TV and in the newspapers. The next year, as part of Friends of the Payette's strategy to give a lasting voice to the Payette and other Idaho waterways, Wendy founded a sibling organization, Idaho Rivers United (IRU). The new group's job was to develop a statewide constituency for rivers to support FOP's efforts with the legislature. Friends of the Payette's steering committee, an extraordinary group of volunteers, hired Liz Paul, top-notch kayaker and seasoned river defender, to organize its legislative campaign.

As if that weren't enough to manage, Wendy's son was born at this time, too. They named him Tommy, because "naming him Payette seemed too hard to explain," Wendy jokes. Still, Tommy was a river baby. He came to the office every day—frequently in a crib T-shirt that had THE PAYETTE RIVER IS NOT FOR SALE inscribed across his tiny chest. For months the baby crawled around happily in an enormous recycling bin while his mom bent the ears of volunteers and legislative aides. Wendy remembers feeling that motherhood was somehow seen as a betrayal to the cause—even though what they were fighting for, really, was protection of a natural wonder for future generations. "When I first told FOP folks that I was pregnant, I felt like it was the ultimate act of disloyalty," she says. "On the other hand, there were a few times after I was showing that I felt my 'condition' was the only reason I wasn't attacked by frustrated loggers at public meetings."

Wendy doesn't even know how the loggers got involved in the first place. This fight wasn't about logging in any way. But it seemed that anything that opposed industry and exploitation of natural resources drew their attention and condemnation, and the Gem project on the North Fork was no exception. As the FOP-organized demonstrations against Gem got under way at the Idaho State Capitol, logging trucks draped banners with anti-preservation sentiments across their loads of cut trees and circled ominously. FOP didn't care. It stuck to its plan and pulled out all the stops. "In some ways what we did was over the top, more audacious than anything

Idaho had seen in a while," Wendy asserts. "Some well-intentioned people thought we were being silly—that the advertising and the rallies and the yard signs were just a bunch of noise." But they worked. One woman legislator asked Wendy why they had put signs in every yard in southwestern Idaho—they were all she could see wherever she turned. Wendy said that was precisely why they had done it.

Gaining High Ground

By 1991 the Water Resources Board was finishing up a draft management plan for the Payette to present to the legislature, just in time for the session. Friends of the Payette had been well represented on its advisory committee by John Wasson. An excellent boater and Hollywood movie consultant, John had worked tirelessly with FOP and IRU to turn out supporters for the board's public hearings. Those were heated, dramatic times, but the public sentiment supporting a free-flowing North Fork was overwhelmingly apparent. No matter how badly the board wanted to side with the industry, members simply couldn't justify it in the face of such opposition. The board had only one choice: to propose to the Idaho Legislature a ban on all hydro development through designation of the North Fork of the Payette as a protected river under Idaho's Protected Rivers Act—the first safety net of its kind.

Gem and its supporters were enraged. Never before had something like this happened in Idaho.

Now the proposal was to be debated on the floor of the Idaho House and Senate. Thanks to the Conservation Alliance grant, FOP could storm the halls of the capitol for real. Everyone donned their dress clothes—even Scott Montgomery. "I was a rock musician and hippie during the 1960s—I'd never owned a real suit, so I had to go buy one. And I learned how to tie a tie on the way to my first lobby visit. But they were messin' with my river, so I did what I had to." Scott's two-week volunteer stint was fast becoming a long-term relationship.

Lobbying was serious business, and Wendy and Scott knew it. Special information materials had to be prepared, requiring countless hours—from a lot of people. Phone banks would have to be organized, and more petitions circulated. Banners and buttons had to be printed. And all the volunteers needed to polish their plea for the Payette. An eight-person lobby team was formed, and together they trained a whole swath of citizen activists to lobby as well. After each visit the team would meet with the volunteers, find out exactly what had taken place during the meeting, then hatch a follow-up plan.

It was a showdown on the Idaho Hill. Wendy was astounded at how many professional lobbyists had been hired by development interests to defeat them. As an act of intimidation, Representative JoAn Wood stood up before the Idaho Resources and Environment Committee—which Wendy fondly refers to as "the Committee of Doom"—and waved a Friends of the Payette brochure in the air. She announced that she was going to find out where all of FOP's money was coming from. The next thing Wendy knew, she was being investigated by the IRS—which turned up nothing incriminating.

During another lobby visit a senator asked, "Does your husband know you're doing this?"

Wendy smiled, then explained that her loving, faithful husband knew all about her love affair with the Payette, and supported it.

Given the sheer number of interests making noise on the issue, the legislators were having a hard time seeing that it had nothing to do with farmers or loggers—many of whom, despite Scott's moderate approach, were arguing that FOP and its counterparts wanted to lock up rivers so no one could irrigate or use electricity. But Friends of the Payette would not back off. It stayed front and center in the media and continued to comb neighborhoods with petitions for support. Every moment that the activists weren't lobbying, they were out collecting signatures.

The Final Push

It was the eleventh hour. Spending just $500, FOP aired a home-made commercial on the local TV station. It was bad, but it got the point across. Then it poured out one final dose of grassroots juice as the bill to save its river was voted upon in the Senate. It had been an extraordinary journey for the group, which now boasted thousands of activists and had done the impossible on a mere $150,000—the only major grant being from the Conservation Alliance. The rest were private donations from individuals and local businesses. Five hundred volunteers had contributed to the effort, and Wendy and Scott cannot say enough about them. "Sometimes I feel badly that Wendy and I got so much credit," Scott laments. "So many people made this happen." And sure enough, as the fate of the North Fork was being debated, a flood of activists descended upon the capitol with 620 letters in support of stopping the hydropower project and protecting the Payette's North Fork from further harm. It was like nothing Idaho's political world had ever seen.

What ultimately convinced the legislators was FOP's message that passing the bill would be a badge of honor: They could actually protect a river *against* the wishes of the federal government! The idea appealed to their anti-fed sentiments, even though messing with western water laws was like shooting a sacred cow. The bill survived the Senate vote. It went on to the House Resources Committee and made it out by only one vote. The floor vote was just as nerve-racking, but the bill squeaked through there as well.

Friends of the Payette had done it. The group had stopped the J. R./Gem dam and ensured that no new water projects would be considered for five years. And it had garnered some additional protection for all of Idaho's rivers through the Idaho Protected Rivers Act.

The legislators' votes, along with the Rivers Act, were intelligent and loving promises made to the people of Idaho. And to the river. They were promises worth keeping.

Reflections and Victories

But as Wendy Wilson says, it's never over. Even in the new millennium, Idaho's river lovers must remain vigilant. They're willing to play that role. "I can never go back again to the person I was before the campaign," Wendy says. "I learned from it how political power works. I learned that if a group of people actually design a campaign correctly, run it seriously, and throw everything they have into it, they can win against tremendous odds. The Payette taught me to expect the best out of myself as an activist."

Wendy has kept her lifelong pledge to the river. She is now working to restore its long-lost chinook salmon, another project funded in part by the Conservation Alliance. It's not lost on Wendy that support of this most recent project is a clear demonstration of the Alliance's long-term commitment to the Payette.

In 1999 there came the fairy-tale ending. Since its legislative defeat, Gem Irrigation had continued its campaign to dam the North Fork by submitting an amended application for a permit that reduced the amount of water it wanted to divert. Friends of the Payette and Idaho Rivers United continued to speak out in opposition, and on October 18, just hours before the permit hearing, Gem withdrew its application—thereby permanently divorcing itself from any opportunity to dam the river, ever. Liz Paul, who had come to the foreground as Wendy and Scott stepped back to reorganize their personal lives, issued a statement: "I look forward to moving the North Fork Payette project to my dead hydro files and enjoying the free-flowing river with my family for years to come. This is a great event for everyone who has fought so hard for the North Fork, and it's an affirmation of our state Protected River system."

Wendy Wilson likens planning for a legislative campaign to preparing a first-aid kit for a river expedition. The morphine and hemostats seem like overkill at first—then suddenly they're indispensable, and you're glad you were prepared. FOP couldn't have saved the North Fork of the Payette without the Conservation Alliance grant, or the yard signs, or massive petition drives and bad TV commercials.

And it couldn't have done it without wholehearted, unconditional commitment. To each other. To themselves. To the Payette. Two sets of vows made over a river. Every woman should be so lucky to have two great loves in her life.

BIBLIOGRAPHY

Bolling, David M. (for River Network). *How to Save a River: A Handbook for Citizen Action*. Washington, D.C.: Island Press, 1994.

Bridges, Marti, and Liz Paul. "Finally the North Fork Payette Is Safe!" *Currently, Idaho Rivers United Newsletter*, winter 2000, 1.

Gallagher, Dan. "From Small Potatoes to Microchips." *Minneapolis Star Tribune*, 4 April 1999.

Idaho Rivers United. *North Fork Payette River Dam Defeated!* www.idahorivers.org, Idaho Rivers United, 1999.

Serwer, Andrew E. "The Simplot Saga: How America's French Fry King Made Billions More in Semiconductors." *Fortune*, 27 November 1995, 68.

Stuebner, Stephen. *Paddling the Payette*. 2nd ed. Boise: Boise Front Adventures, 1998.

Wilson, Wendy. "How Idaho Learned to Say Yes to Rivers." Boise, 1998. Photocopy of unpublished article.

A Gift of Red Rock

Dugout Ranch, Utah
1992–1997

The blood red walls of Indian Creek Basin rose from the sandstone rubble. Like clenched fists, they shot straight into a vast desert sky. Beneath them was hardly a human imprint—save the ruins of the ancient Native People. There were no strip malls. No convenience stores. No Motel 6. And only one paved road for miles.

But it was about to change.

Chris Montague kept one eye on the road and the other on the view. He had always loved the drive between these nine-hundred-foot sandstone cliffs—it served as foreground to a panorama so massive, it was almost incomprehensible in scale. To the south he could see the Abajo Mountains, harboring thick forests and herds of elk. Ahead, the horizon was anchored by two nippled monoliths—North and South Six-Shooter Peaks. Just beyond them lay the incised labyrinths and jade-colored Colorado River in Canyonlands National Park.

As he came into view of the Dugout Ranch, his knuckles paled on the steering wheel.

What if they couldn't pull it off? What if this lovely fertile basin, home of the Dugout and the very marrow of the Colorado Plateau, was to be churned into condominiums? Or a golf course? Chris knew the facts: If he, the Utah Nature Conservancy's director of conservation programs, couldn't strike a deal with the Redd family, the ranch's owners, he could kiss this entire region goodbye. For it seemed as though every real estate developer both east and west of the Mississippi was waiting to get a hold of the ranch.

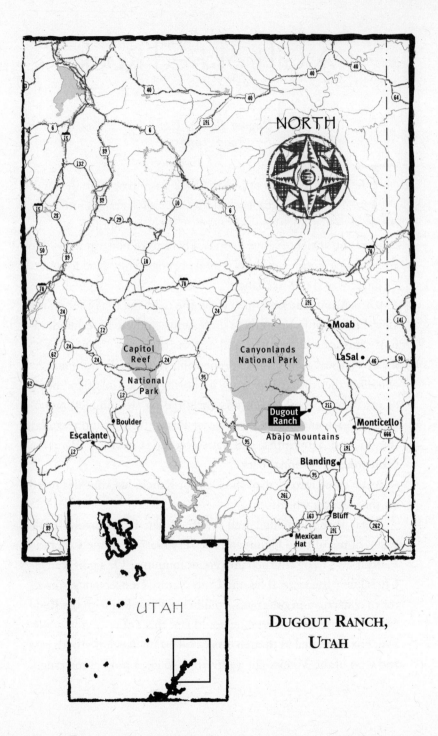

NORTH

Moab

LaSal

Capitol
Reef

National
Park

Canyonlands
National Park

Dugout
Ranch

Monticello

Abajo Mountains

Boulder

Blanding

Escalante

Bluff

Mexican
Hat

UTAH

DUGOUT RANCH,
UTAH

The ranch property itself wasn't so important—although it did house historic structures of an earlier, wilder West and was a showcase for environmentally sensitive ranching practices. What was critical was that the ranch served as a kind of connective tissue for a larger, less tame body of land deep in Utah's canyon country. It served as a wildlife corridor. It provided water. And it guarded an unbroken view that rocked the soul.

Despite its magnitude, Chris knew how easily disturbed the sandstone deserts were—that much he'd discovered as a boy exploring southeastern Utah's topography. He had learned that a single footprint could crush an entire community of organisms— tiny cryptobiotics that hold the nutrients and moisture required for plant life to survive. If trampled, these tiny colonies took nearly a hundred years to recover. Flash floods were common—although water was scarce. In a single summer thunderstorm, huge amounts of water would collect on the smooth sandstone cliffs, then pour off with violent velocity. Charging into washes and canyons, it scoured the landscape, snatching anything in its path. Boulders, trees, and jackrabbits were all sealed in a coffin of mud as the flood slowed to a stop.

A Target for Pleasure and Profit

The fragile, uncertain nature of this place was why Chris and the Redds were fending off the developers who were scratching at the back door. Robert and Heidi Redd had recently divorced, and word was out that the family was trying to divide its assets. The former couple and their two sons dreaded the developers, and heaven knew the ranch couldn't handle much more attention than it was already getting. The area was crawling with people; thanks to a booming economy and media hits in the *New York Times* and *USA Today*, folks were looking to snatch up land in Utah's canyon country for commercial development and the building of second homes. Given the dwindling profits from raising cattle on austere desert lands, ranchers were especially vulnerable to the overtures of real estate agents. If the shortsighted were to get their hands on Dugout, the pastoral ranch and majestic land around it could easily become the same kind of cluttered gateway as the West Entrance to Yellowstone Park. It was a grim visual in Chris Montague's mind.

Chris and the Redds weren't the only ones fretting over the future of the ranch. Walt Dabney, superintendent of the adjacent

Visitors ride the range at Dugout Ranch.

Canyonlands National Park at the time, stated that "the setting makes the ranch a potential subdivision target, and such development, which could include facilities such as golf courses and condominiums, would seriously change the rugged open spaces that now characterize the approach to the park. Development would also require large amounts of limited available water and reduce critical wildlife access in riparian areas." Tourism and recreation were also affecting the area. By 1990 low gas prices and an increase in Americans' disposable income meant visits to southern Utah's national parks had increased by 10 percent in each of the past ten years—and neighboring Canyonlands was no exception. At least seven hotels had been built in the nearby towns of Monticello and Moab, and more campers than ever were accessing the public lands around the ranch for the free campsites they offered. Rock climbing especially had exploded as a recreational opportunity, and soon the walls of Indian Creek were lathered with human bodies. Given the sheer number of them, the footpaths they etched into the soft hillsides were becoming visible.

For the time being it wasn't an overwhelming task to keep developers at bay. Nor to accommodate a growing number of rock climbers—who mostly regulated themselves. But Heidi Redd had no idea how to deal with the off-road vehicles that were running rampant on the public lands around her; they were ravaging the delicate desert soils and crushing various plants and animals at an unprecedented rate. In the state of Utah alone, registration of these machines had more than tripled in the last decade. So agile and rugged were the new models that the recreationists who drove them were getting into places never before traveled. In the process, "relic" or presettlement plant communities were uprooted, and archaeological sites were flattened. Entire slopes were denuded by the churning tires, causing erosion and runoff problems in the ranch's streambeds. The glistening slime of two-stroke engine oil could be seen on the water's surface. And the adjoining public lands that had been determined to have wilderness character—largely because they were roadless and offered opportunities for solitude—now had so many tire tracks across them that they looked like a plate of spaghetti.

Too many hands wanted to help themselves to the treasures of the Indian Creek corridor and Dugout Ranch.

So when Heidi walked into The Nature Conservancy's Salt Lake office on South Temple, she asked to see Chris and listed the current threats to her family's property and the lands around it. "I can see the writing on the wall," she said. "And my family's situation isn't going to help. The place is getting loved to death and it's only going to get worse." She took off her cowboy hat and placed it in her lap. "Can you help?"

Chris understood that the Dugout Ranch was threatened—the family needed to sell to split the assets among the former spouses and their two sons. He also knew that Dugout stood as a powerful symbol for the canyon country of southern Utah's Colorado Plateau. Known for its slickrock, the region has seen microbrews and mountain bikes named in its honor. Almost every sport-utility vehicle ad under the sun had been shot on its terra-cotta terra firma. There was no doubt about it—this region was one of the last great American landscapes.

The End of an Era

Like every Utahan, Chris knew about Heidi, the cowgirl of canyon country. He'd heard tales of her life—like the one about a bear breaking into her house in the middle of the night. She lassoed the animal and dragged it into a horse trailer. He could imagine Heidi riding the range of Indian Creek—long before the coyotes' night song faded into the sunrise, before the camping climbers got their coffee pots to a rolling boil. In the saddle her long blond braids would swing from beneath a ten-gallon hat that was almost as big as she was. In her late fifties, Heidi still drove cattle with her hired hands, sleeping in line cabin shacks for nights on end with nothing but a bedroll and a few cans of chili. She branded and castrated calves alongside the men. The mother of two sons and a highly respected range manager who served on the board of the Public Lands Council of the National Cattlemen's Beef Association, Heidi Redd ran Dugout Ranch, smack in the middle of Indian Creek basin.

In 1992, on that first day in Chris's office on South Temple, she explained to him the history of Dugout, which foretold how the family had landed in its current dilemma. She boasted of a fine cattle operation, saying that the land was in better shape than in the old days, when the ranch was owned by the Scorup-

Somerville outfit—one of the largest cattle ranching operations in Utah. That was before 1965, when pioneer cattleman Charlie Redd, the father of her ex-husband Robert, bought out Scorup-Somerville. At the time the old guard had two thousand head running on its allotments. But Charlie had acquired the Dugout parcel only as part of a larger deal; he really had his sights on 17,000 acres of the ranch that were located in the nearby La Sal Mountains. Charlie prepared to sell Dugout on the open market, but his son Robert, with Heidi as his new bride, intercepted. They traded their part in the larger family operation for sole ownership of Dugout, a 5,000-plus-acre ranch that included 250,000 acres of grazing permits on the adjoining public lands. Shouldering an enormous debt, which Heidi figures would amount to a couple of million dollars today, the newlyweds taught themselves the ranching business.

There were new tricks to learn. Heidi and Robert wanted to raise cattle in a way that was less damaging to the land they loved. Besides, they figured it made better business sense to have a healthy range. Eventually they succeeded in creating an operation more conservation minded than their predecessors had; they ran fewer cattle, maintained native grasses, and worked to restore and maintain the critical riparian corridor of Indian Creek.

For many years the desert ranching lifestyle was a satisfying one for Heidi and Robert Redd. But they barely survived some early disasters. On their first Christmas a blizzard struck while their cattle were fenced in at 8,000 feet in the high country of Dark Canyon Plateau. The young couple headed up into the hills and for six miles never saw a fence or road, because the snow was so deep. On snowmobiles they hauled what hay they could to keep the herd from starving. They tried to save the freezing, hungry cattle, but lost three hundred head in the process.

Finally the erratic cycles of desert droughts and blizzards, coupled with fluctuating beef prices, took their toll. After twenty-three years of marriage, Heidi and Robert found themselves in divorce court. Robert wanted to be rid of the business; he moved to Virginia and remarried. After buying out his half of the cattle, Heidi remained at the ranch.

Very quickly Heidi and her two sons realized that the ranch couldn't sustain three families, and the boys investigated ranching opportunities on their own. Heidi struggled with the downward spiral of desert ranching economics. Everyone was looking for a way out.

Heidi's weathered face stared hard at Chris. There seemed no way to hold the ranch together, she said. They had to sell. Besides real estate developers, agents for well-heeled celebrities like Ralph Lauren and Christie Brinkley had made known their interest in the ranch, but no one was certain what they intended to do with the property. Other ranchers, less green than the Redds, salivated over the grazing allotments. And there were those in the county who wanted the precious water rights to Indian Creek—which Dugout controlled. So many threats, she said. So many threats.

Then she named her price. It was miles beyond anything The Nature Conservancy of Utah had ever taken on. Chris shook his head and said sorry; that kind of purchase was out of the group's league.

The Wealth of Dugout

But Dugout lingered in the back of his mind. Eventually he decided to take a trip down to the ranch itself. Through the core of the basin, across the ranch property, he saw that Indian Creek and its tributaries gently carved perennial, 42-mile routes through verdant clusters of cottonwoods and willows—a significant feat in the second driest state in the nation. He could easily see this was the main artery of life for not just the ranch but an entire landscape.

Chris knew that Dugout was the only significant block of private property within hundreds of square miles. With the exception of some state inholdings, the surrounding land was public domain managed for the benefit of all Americans and their future generations. The responsibility for this stewardship on the public's behalf was in the hands of three federal agencies—the U.S. Forest Service, the Bureau of Land Management (BLM), and the National Park Service. Beyond its 5,167 privately owned acres, Dugout Ranch possessed grazing permits that allowed it to run cattle on the surrounding Forest Service and BLM lands. What affected Dugout would affect an entire body of prized public terrain. The ranch really was the critical connection.

The Dugout property and surrounding lands sustain a wealth of wildlife and serve as home to at least four globally rare plants.

When he got back to the city, Chris shared his observations with the Utah Conservancy's state director, Dave Livermore. A veteran conservationist of nearly twenty years, Dave was intrigued by the significance of the ranch, both ecologically and culturally— he had a special interest in working with local communities and economies. A southern Utah ranching operation sounded like an appealing partnership for The Nature Conservancy to pursue.

Dave and Chris gathered their scientific staff and initiated an inventory of the property's biological resources. "We couldn't believe what we found," Chris says. "There were at least four globally rare plants: kachina and alcove rock daisies, and Tuhy's breadroot and pinnate spring parsley. The water source was sustaining black bears, cougars, and wild turkeys—and supporting an important winter range for deer. There were redtails, balds, goldens, and peregrine falcons. We found that 80 percent of the wildlife occurred within one mile of Indian Creek and its tributaries, which underscored the importance of maintaining the creek. And we discovered that it was an archaeological treasure chest. I mean, there were thousands of sites."

In the Anasazi petroglyphs on the walls above the ruins, what the staff noticed were the hands. Some figures were carved gripping spears and shields; others clutched thunderbolts or enormous snakes. Some stood with their hands open. Some hands were raised upward, toward the sun. All were demonstrations of the power of people comingling with the power of nature—two forces joined by place and time. The artwork was the essence of the Indian Creek basin, a place shaped by people.

Environmentalists or Ranchers?

But the presence of people had taken its toll. Ancient cliff dwellers and contemporary climbers were one thing, but cows were a real problem. Many Utah conservationists, like Chip Ward, were skeptical about saving any southern Utah ranch—arguing that cows, no matter how well managed, had no business grazing the West's fragile, arid lands. In his book *Canaries on the Rim*, Chip writes, "Although the landscape of California and much of the rest of the West looks 'normal' to us today, it is not what it once was . . . we deny our history and are reluctant to face and fix the mistakes we made when we tried to impose the wet European paradigm of cows in pastures on a vast and dry western landscape."

But Dave and Chris saw that, compared to other Utah ranching operations, Dugout Ranch was exemplary. Under Heidi and Robert's stewardship, nature and culture had lived hand in hand in the Indian Creek corridor. As long as bovines and their beef remained part of western economics, why couldn't the property become a model for other ranchers to draw inspiration from? And if The Nature Conservancy could acquire the property, it would be able to educate other land users to tread more lightly.

Making the Connection

While they had seen much impact, many of the public lands adjoining the ranch still maintained a pristine character and had been congressionally proposed for wilderness designation under the 1964 Wilderness Act. So unique and spectacular is this region that, over half a century ago, Wilderness Society founder Bob Marshall proposed additional protection for these public lands—spanning the entire Canyonlands basin from rim to rim—before the Wilderness Act had been adopted by Congress. The national monument would have reached from Escalante in central Utah to Moab near the state's eastern border. It would have embraced 4.5 million acres of silent and wild terrain.

But powerful development interests, whose eagerness for mining and oil and gas exploration outweighed concern for national treasures, heavily lobbied western senators and congressmen. Twice the decision makers shot down Marshall's proposal—in 1936 and again in 1961, when Secretary of the Interior Stewart Udall called for the creation of an 800,000-acre, rim-to-rim Canyonlands National Park. By the time Canyonlands was finally set aside by Congress in 1964, the same year that the Wilderness Act was passed, it was a measly 257,000 acres—less than 6 percent of the original proposal and hardly representative of the rich diversity of terrain and species that characterized the region. In recent times the park boundary has been described by one park official as having a "bathtub ring" around it; without extended park protection or wilderness designation for the excluded public lands at its edge, those lands could be degraded by overuse and lack of management, while the token island of park land remained pristine. Such a plan lacked any real purpose in the larger scheme of ecosystem protection—and a dearth of adequate protection to deserving, surrounding lands made it even more critical that Dugout Ranch remain undeveloped.

Knowing what they now knew, Chris and Dave, along with the rest of the Conservancy staff, realized they couldn't walk away— no matter what the price. This place was far too important to cede to developers or overzealous recreationists. So with the results of the natural resource inventory, they went back to Heidi Redd and agreed to try to buy the property—with the understanding that she would remain on the premises and run the ranch for at least another ten years.

The Settlement

If they had known what they were getting into, the parties may never have agreed to enter negotiations. Round after round of discussion ensued, with Chris and Dave acting as diplomatic diehards. Chris remembers how much distrust Robert and the two sons initially had in both the process and the Conservancy. After all, for western ranchers, conservationists were usually the enemy. The Conservancy staff did everything they could to develop an atmosphere of confidence among the Redd clan, which included sending the two younger men to a working ranch purchased by the Wyoming chapter of the organization to see how the Conservancy had preserved its traditions. "Sometimes we'd get together and there would be four or five lawyers in the room, each representing a separate interest," Chris recalls. "You can imagine how slowly things went." They'd reach the point where they thought they had a settlement—and *boom*, one of the legal eagles would blow it up.

The negotiations continued for four years.

"It was exhausting for all of us and very traumatic for the family. I was so impressed that everyone hung in there after the thing fell apart so many times," Chris says. Dave agrees, adding, "But what made it happen was each family member shared with us a common vision to protect the ranch from development. And that was the glue that held us together. It wasn't all about money."

And at the end of the arduous process, as everyone was pulling their pens from their pockets to sign a purchase agreement, one of the Redds suddenly recalled five horses that had originally lived on the ranch but hadn't been divided among them—although all had died or been sold off some time before. The mere memory of the animals threatened to detonate the entire agreement. In a desperate last-minute gesture, the Conservancy staff offered to purchase the missing horses to restore the lost equilibrium—a most unusual expenditure for a nonprofit group to make. But with five phantom horses in tow, the deal finally had the green light.

In September 1996—on the very day that President Clinton recognized the significance of Utah's canyon country by proclaiming the Grand Staircase–Escalante National Monument in the central part of the state—the Conservancy signed a one-year option to buy. But unlike the executive order that established the new monument—which opponents labeled a "land grab"—the Dugout Ranch partnership received broad, bipartisan support. Utah governor Mike Leavitt spoke at the signing of the option, and demonstrated his lack of understanding about land protection by commenting, "Now this [Dugout Ranch] is a *real* monument"—as if there could be any real land protection without both public and private land preservation. Indeed, that was the whole point of protecting Dugout. The *Salt Lake Tribune*, which usually supported industry and development over any environmental efforts, gave the one-year option a nod of approval; its editorial opinion praised the option as holding "the promise of preserving both the land and a traditional lifestyle," adding that "it is an

Saddling up beneath a sandstone butte, Dugout Ranch.

admirable compromise between the ideals of ecological preservation and an income-producing business."

Paying the Bill

But the fun had just begun. Although it had successfully completed seventy-two land protection projects, preserving some 276,000 acres statewide, acquiring Dugout was a daunting prospect for

The Nature Conservancy of Utah—given the asking price and the number of players involved. It was by far the largest Conservancy project in Utah history and a complicated deal to boot.

And the clock was ticking. The Conservancy had to come up with $4.6 million to purchase the ranch. It also needed funds for conservation start-up costs—for instance, to purchase fencing for threatened areas. Organizational policy ensured the long-term health of the project by requiring that the group raise a percentage of the overall price to implement an endowment fund, too. The overall ticket price was more than $6 million.

The Utah Conservancy staff—just eight people, led by Dave Livermore—pulled together an aggressive fund-raising strategy, seeking lead gifts from prominent Utah foundations to get the momentum going before turning to the public. The George S. and Dolores Dore Eccles Foundation got the ball rolling with an unprecedented contribution of just over a million dollars. But the grant was given in the form of a challenge pledge: Twenty-five dollars would be doled out for each hundred-dollar bill contributed by an individual.

So enamored was it with the richness and beauty of the region that the Conservancy's home office moved the project to the top of its acquisitions list and kicked in another million from the president's own discretionary fund. With nearly $2.5 million in hand, the project was off to an auspicious beginning. Next the group turned to a handful of wealthy individuals. Making dozens of trips to the site, Heidi joined the staff in taking prospective donors on horseback to see the treasures of Dugout and the surrounding public lands depending on it. Libby Ellis, formerly of the California-based Patagonia company and an ex–board member of the Outdoor Industry Conservation Alliance (OICA), was now sitting on the other side of the conservation fence as development director for The Nature Conservancy of Utah. She recounts one ranch trip: "A flock of sandhill cranes flew over us in perfect formation. They circled our heads, and we stood there in sheer amazement—

I mean, sandhill cranes in the desert? There was something so powerful about such an unlikely scene—we just knew then that the project would happen." Sure enough, through such trips and one-on-one efforts, another $1.5 million was secured.

But the deepest pockets had all been dug from, and Libby and the rest of the staff were still several million dollars away from their goal. The year was fading fast and the option to buy would soon expire.

It was time to water the grassroots. Special mailings went out to Conservancy members, and media outreach was accomplished in the few spare minutes the staff could glean from their long days in the office and out in the field. Through their labors and some luck, the project caught the attention of the *New York Times*. Featuring Heidi Redd, the story of the lone cowgirl and her canyon country home touched the hearts of Americans everywhere. The donations poured into the office like a flash flood, eroding away the amount they still needed.

Libby Ellis had been in this business long enough to know where to look for additional funds. And as a veteran climber herself, she knew how much Indian Creek meant to outdoor enthusiasts—especially those with a vertical bent. So she returned to her old stomping grounds with a proposal in hand for the Outdoor Industry Conservation Alliance.

John Sterling remembers the proposal well, saying that it generated heated and lengthy discussion among Alliance board members. The project was proposed by The Nature Conservancy—a big organization with a lot more resources than the little local groups that the OICA typically supported. Wouldn't its money be more useful if given to a small, scrappy group? And some of the groups within the Alliance were concerned with the fat sticker price of Dugout. But John, a former front-line activist who serves on the Alliance board, argued that "fifty years from now nobody will care what it cost. The place will endure far beyond the memory of the expense."

The Conservation Alliance was forced to think hard about its funding criteria. In the end it took a big-picture view: This was big acreage next to even bigger acreage—adjacent to national parks, wilderness areas, and proposed wilderness areas. The project meant true habitat protection.

The proposal went from an initial near-rejection by the board to winning more votes than any other proposal that funding cycle. John says, "That's what's cool about the Conservation Alliance— we are willing to bend our own rules for the right reasons." Shortly thereafter, the Conservancy's Utah staff received a check for $35,000 from the Alliance, bringing them one step closer to their final goal.

Vertical Verve

But what was more important about the OICA support was that it sparked great interest in the outdoor recreation community. One group in particular took notice of the Conservancy's effort. As soon as they heard about it, climbers everywhere were horrified at the potential paving and taming of Dugout—a place that had provided so many ascents steeped in silence amid magical vistas. The towering walls of Indian Creek and the ranch below were an icon of the American climbing scene, featured in equipment catalogs and in such magazines as *Outside* and *Climbing*. The thought of trying to climb next to tourist shops and an IMAX theater was unbearable—and hopeless if the new owners cut off access to some of the community's most beloved climbs. So The Access Fund, a climbers' organization that seeks to protect climbing resources, rolled up its sleeves and got to work. Its staff and volunteers sent out alerts to the fund's 7,000-plus members nationwide and organized trail building and maintenance near the Indian Creek cliffs, in a gesture of support and respect for the area. They raised $1,000 and encouraged members to donate more. Black Diamond, a Utah-based manufacturer of climbing and mountaineering equipment, publicized the plight of Dugout in its international mail-order catalog and donated another $1,000. Peter Metcalf, its CEO and a well-respected climber and businessman, sent a letter to his corporate connections in the industry and asked them to hand over support as well. It was a fabulous joining of the hands of outdoor enthusiasts across the country.

Erosion continued.

Thanks to the volunteer efforts of cowboys, climbers, and other citizens, more than 6,000 individual donations spilled into the Conservancy's Utah headquarters. "The postman could barely get in our front door, he was so loaded down," Libby Ellis recalls. The checks came with letters, many from people who had never seen the place but understood its worth. Others were moved by Heidi's hope and vision. One older couple had honeymooned in Canyonlands and remembered the ranch from their photo album. Young climbers in the East were saving their money so they could come to Utah and scale the great red walls above Dugout. When they finally made the pilgrimage, they wanted to see the place intact—the way it was pictured in the magazines. One redrock climber from nearby Cortez, Colorado, started his own grassroots campaign for Dugout. After an intensive schedule presenting slide shows throughout the southern portion of his state, he proudly added $2,000 more to the pot.

The Geography of Hope

In September 1997 The Nature Conservancy announced that it had met its goal. Together the Conservancy and Heidi Redd would manage Dugout's natural and cultural resources. That summer over a thousand people gathered together at Dugout Ranch to celebrate its preservation. The smoky scent of barbecue drifted in the air, and birds of prey made winged shadows on the cliff faces above the basin. People took in the expanse around them—an expanse they had helped preserve. The son and granddaughter of Wallace Stegner were present. As one of the West's greatest literary figures, Stegner had written that southern Utah was "the geography of hope." And indeed it was a hopeful day. A day that spanned the generations. A joining of hands. A gift of redrock given in perpetuity.

Later on Dave Livermore joined Heidi at a celebration in Manhattan's Central Park—a black-tie affair to benefit The Nature Conservancy nationwide. There Heidi was honored with the Wallace Stegner Conservation Award before a thousand people including Tom Brokaw, Dan Rather, and numerous other big guns. Heidi pulled off her ten-gallon hat and tossed it high into the urban air. She let out a whoop and shouted, "This is enough to scare the *shit* outta any cowgirl!"

The Indian Creek basin remains as it has always been—full of rattlesnakes and rabbitbrush. It remains the connective tissue for canyon country.

Climbers still dot the blood red walls, and Heidi's herd of cattle still roams the range. Indian Creek flows freely through the basin. And the cowgirl remains in the saddle, her gnarled, sandstone-colored fingers still holding a rope and branding iron. "I'll be out there riding until I'm ninety," she has been known to say.

After the last paper was signed, Chris Montague drove his family down to see the ranch and all that it held together. He exhaled a sigh of satisfaction as long as the Colorado River. All of them, together. They'd done it. They'd really done it.

The ghosts of the Anasazi must be pleased. Among the rustle of the cottonwoods and the murmurs of Indian Creek, Chris could almost hear their applause.

BIBLIOGRAPHY

Dabney, Walter D., Superintendent of Canyonlands National Park. Letter to Nature Conservancy Board, 1 December 1995.

Nature Conservancy of Utah. *The Dugout Ranch Conservation Project: Preserving Wildlife and a Way of Life in Utah's Canyonlands.* Salt Lake City: Nature Conservancy of Utah, 1996.

Salt Lake City Deseret News, 1–24 September 1996.

Salt Lake Tribune, 1 September 1996–7 February 1997.

Utah Wilderness Coalition. *Wilderness at the Edge: A Citizen Proposal to Protect Utah's Canyons and Deserts.* Salt Lake City: Utah Wilderness Coalition, 1990.

Ward, Chip. *Canaries on the Rim: Living Downwind in the West.* New York: Verso, 1999.

Wild at Heart

The Tatshenshini River. The very epitome of North American wilderness. Hardly accessible and fed by chalky glacial till, the river is the color of veins beneath skin. It is buried deep in the North, where Alaska, British Columbia, and the Yukon converge—a place where some of the wildest terrain on the planet comes together.

In the late 1980s the Tatshenshini was still a mystery to most. Even as the twentieth century faded on the horizon, hardly anyone in the so-called civilized world had ever heard of it. Except a mining company and a few boaters.

The pulse of its waters is enough to move mountains—and it has. It is a restless region; in 1899 the largest earthquake in North America was recorded here, just north of the river. It measured 8.6 on the Richter scale. In only five minutes—a nanosecond in geologic time—the surrounding St. Elias Mountains shot up an additional fifty feet, and their ice fields were thrust outward half a mile.

And just forty-seven years earlier, the Tatshenshini region had pounded and throbbed until a wall of blue ice burst from its ancient bearings. A 50-mile-long lake that had been dammed by the ice wall was released. The Native People who lived down in the river valley looked up to see a half-mile-high wall of water pumping toward them.

Those who survived retreated to the river's mouth, on the Pacific Ocean. Their descendants ventured up the Tatshenshini

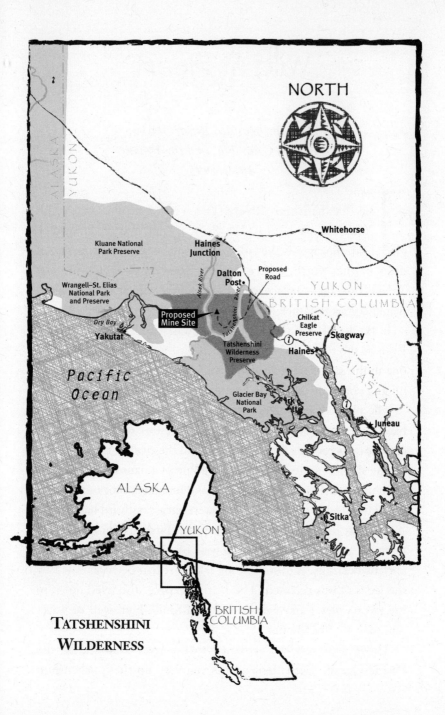

NORTH

Whitehorse

Kluane National
Park Preserve

Haines
Junction

Dalton
Post•

Proposed
Road

Alsek River

YUKON

BRITISH COLUMBIA

Wrangell–St. Elias
National Park
and Preserve

Dry Bay

Proposed
Mine Site

Tatshenshini River

Chilkat
Eagle
Preserve

Skagway

Yakutat

Tatshenshini
Wilderness
Preserve

ⓘ

Haines

Pacific
Ocean

Glacier Bay
National
Park

rk
te

ALASKA

ⓘ

Juneau

ALASKA

YUKON

Sitka

BRITISH
COLUMBIA

**TATSHENSHINI
WILDERNESS**

only to fish or hunt. No one wanted to face again the furious beatings of such an uncontainable, arrhythmic heart.

The pulse of these waters is enough to stir people, too—into doing the most outrageous things. In the late 1980s Geddes Resources, a mining corporation from Toronto, submitted a proposal to the Canadian government. It wanted to decapitate Windy Craggy, a magnificent, 6,000-foot peak that loomed over the Tatshenshini River. From the open wound replacing its summit, the company wanted to drain the mountain of the rich copper ore that coursed through its veins. The process could poison the Tatshenshini and effectively end one of the North American coast's most prominent salmon runs. Other animals depended upon these fish for survival as well: grizzly bears, bald eagles, the elusive and rare glacier bear, wolves. The process would have stopped the heartbeat of an entire region.

Then there were those who wanted to boat the Tat's spirited, vascular waters—but unlike the mine, in this effort they were a threat only to themselves. In 1972 one Walt Blackadar became the first kayaker to paddle solo through the region's forbidding Turnback Canyon, which runs into the Tat from the Alsek River. While he ran its Class V rapids, a level of white-water paddled by only a brave few, the river pulled him under the massive tongue of the Tweedmuir Glacier; he rode beneath it on a bucking current until it spit him out downstream—miraculously still alive. Today kayakers make a helicopter portage to avoid Turnback. Later Blackadar penned these words in a journal-style article for *Sports Illustrated*: "Unbelievable . . . I'm not coming back. Not for $50,000. Not for all the tea in China. Read my words well and don't be a fool. It's unpaddleable."

Unpaddleable. Uncontainable. Perhaps unknowable. Still, the Tat got known fast, thanks to Geddes's plans. It began very simply: with one river rat and one tree hugger. And a lot of heart.

A Boater with a Mission

Johnny Mikes Junior, a partner in Canada's oldest rafting company, first ran the Tatshenshini in 1977. After that he ran many commercial trips on the river—it was his favorite run. No other wilderness was as expansive, as untouched; no other river was as full of verve. In 1987 the browned and brawny guide hit up Ric Careless, a wilderness activist with an impressive campaign record in British Columbia, to join him on the Tat's waters. Mikes promised Careless the wilderness experience of a lifetime. It was a bold claim to make to someone already intimately acquainted with the wildest parts of B.C. and the Yukon.

"I'll give you the trip for free," Mikes said.

That sounded pretty appealing to a guy who made his living keeping other things alive—not a career that featured a lot of pay. But Careless suspected that Mikes was doing more than being generous; he had heard that the Tat was under siege by a mining company making noise on an archaic mining claim. Careless was reluctant to get sucked into the fight, because he was drained after an intense battle to save Height of the Rockies—which to his credit finally rested in perpetual protection. Bleeding-heart tree hugger that he was, Careless knew he wouldn't be able to say no to the cause.

But Mikes was relentless. After two years Careless finally gave in to the young man's earnest pleas and agreed to go. In 1989, semirecovered from the last battle, he flew north to meet Mikes and found himself in the middle of 2.4 million acres of roadless terrain. Here the Tatshenshini coursed from its deep chambers in the subarctic interior all the way to the marine lowlands.

The Topography of the Tat

So undisturbed was this obscure part of Canada, tucked into the Alaskan panhandle, that it was still unknown to many British Columbians. And the only reason it hadn't been developed was that access was so difficult. After all, it was Crown Land—which was managed for "multiple use," much like American public lands under the care of the Bureau of Land Management (BLM). Unfortunately, as on BLM lands, *multiple use* often translated to "abuse"; preservation and recreation seemed to go out the window when there was oil, ore, or timber to be had, especially if it was on land the public didn't know much about.

The Tat is embraced by lands afforded far better protection: Glacier Bay and Wrangell–St. Elias National Parks in Alaska, and Kluane National Park in the Yukon. The river winds its way

The Tatshenshini and Alsek Rivers provide the only access through the 400-mile-long St. Elias mountain range.

through the ice castles of the inland until it joins with the Alsek River, whose upper half is guarded within the boundaries of the Kluane Park. Together they create a pleated, mile-wide waterway that pierces the 400-mile-long, 3-mile-high St. Elias range before uniting with the Pacific Ocean. The river corridor is the only access through the St. Elias; salmon, coastal bears, and Native anglers all pass through this ventricle to access it.

The St. Elias Mountains are as impressive as the Tat and the Alsek. The highest coastal mountains on the planet, they are home to three of North America's four tallest peaks. Their glaciers are massive—no others of this size exist outside the polar zones. Because of their extreme vertical relief—which can exceed even that found in the Himalayas—these peaks are treasures to the mountaineering elite. As other mountain ranges in the world have become overrun with peak baggers and discarded oxygen bottles, first ascents and ski descents here have become increasingly in vogue. The tradition began in style: In 1867 the Duke of Abruzzi journeyed from Italy to be the first on Mount St. Elias's summit. With him came porters who dragged a 700-pound sled, which included a brass bed for their royal ringleader.

The Seduction

Mikes put the group in at Dalton Post, named for an old gold swindler. Over the next twelve days, they would run the river's 160-mile course until it deposited their raft at Dry Bay on the Alaskan coast. Immediately Careless was seduced. Mikes described to him how each autumn the Tat runs blood red with spawning sockeye salmon; how the bears and raptors and wolves embark on a feeding frenzy that makes them the healthiest specimens anywhere. But on that day the river flashed silver with thirty-pound chinook. Old-growth trees lined the riverbank, with dozens of bald eagles decorating them like origami ornaments. Moist maritime winds rode up the waterway, inspiring abundant and nourishing vegetation for the bears, Dall sheep, and mountain goats. It was no surprise to Careless that this region held the world's densest concentration of grizzly dens. What was wondrous to him was catching sight of a glacier bear standing in what is its only home on the planet. This exceptionally uncommon species of bear has smoke-blue fur, and that day it shimmered in the sun much like the Tatshenshini itself.

On the first afternoon, as they steered the raft toward a beach pegged for camp, a grizzly and two cubs strolled out onto it. The collective mass of the animals overshadowed the thirty yards of sandbar. Standing in the eddy, the sow caught a chinook, the water swirling with scarlet scarves of blood as her claws buried into its side. She wrestled it to the beach, where she and her young feasted on its hearty flesh. Leaving entrails and bones behind, the family then lumbered back into the brush and up the hillside in search of soapberries for dessert. A pair of eagles descended to pick at the scraps; a raven landed nearby to protest their good fortune. A wolf stepped out of the boreal forest and circled once around the beach to see if there was enough to go around. Disappointed, he slipped back into the brush the way he'd come. By the time Careless's group set foot on the sandbar, the only evidence of the gathering was in the mud: a calligraphy of animal tracks and the imprints of the chinook's head and tail—made as it thrashed back and forth in its final struggle with the grizz. In all his days in wild places, this was the most concentrated, complete collection of wildlife Careless had ever seen.

The Tatshenshini sustained all of it.

Not If, but When

But Careless's elation was clouded by the neon orange survey tape that fluttered from tree trunks and bushes as they floated by. It was an aberration here. Mikes grit his teeth at the flags as he described what Geddes planned to do to the wild place that surrounded them.

The company's engineers had discovered Windy Craggy's copper lode in the 1960s, but that era's technology and economics couldn't justify its extraction. By the 1980s, however, a good economy and the well-spun illusion that technology could accomplish anything, anywhere, jump-started Geddes's development of the claim. The company submitted to the Canadian government a proposal that included shearing the peak off Windy Craggy and transforming it into an open-pit mine that would generate 30,000 tons of copper daily, along with 375 million tons of waste rock and tailings—the earthen debris left behind after completion of the mining operation. The company planned to ship the ore concentrate through a slurry pipeline—but in order to build the pipeline and the mining village, the proposal called for a high-grade road to be bladed through 70 miles of bear, wolf, Dall sheep, moose, and eagle habitat. The road would cross a series of bridges that would stand like vise grips over the Tatshenshini River, puncturing breeding sites for trumpeter swans and gyrfalcons. The orange ribbons marked the road's path of destruction.

Geddes was quoted as saying that the impacts from their mining operation "would be negligible."

Negligent was probably a better word. The mountain's copper was up to 40 percent sulfide, a substance that generates sulfuric acid, or battery acid, when exposed to air. Sulfide also causes heavy metals to leach from the bedrock. This combination—acid and heavy metal—is lethal to fish, and could in turn wipe out the wildlife communities that depend upon the fish for sustenance.

The disaster wasn't a question of *if* but rather of *when*. Despite Geddes's statements that its "state-of-the-art" facility would not produce acid, the most recent industry report, delivered just two years earlier at the Canadian Acid Mine Drainage Seminar in 1987, concluded with the statement, "The authors know of no massive sulfide mines which have not become acid producers." And a government report asserted, "Exposed tailings left along stream and river banks after a dam breach would continue to generate acidity and metals in solution indefinitely. Destruction of fish habitat would be essentially permanent."

This was bad news not only for the bears and other creatures but also for the fishing industry. The Alsek and Tatshenshini Rivers support commercial, subsistence, and sport fisheries valued at more than $8.5 million annually. And trashing the place would have harmed the river-running industry.

Sweet Talk

But Geddes pointed out that the mine would operate for only fifteen years. It soothed initial concerns, saying that reclamation procedures would return the mine to conditions similar to its present state. However dead fish, a roaded hillside, and a ravaged mountaintop were hardly reclaimable. The grizzly bears would have to abandon the dens that the road took over, and without their food source, their future looked bleak. Even more so for the glacier bear, which had no other home.

Geddes had a solution for disposal of the acid and heavy-metal toxins. It proposed storing the waste rock and tailings underwater, in a 2.5-mile-long reservoir just 3 miles from where the Alsek joined the Tatshenshini. Geddes assured government officials that company engineers had designed a storage lake sure to withstand any geologic event for thousands of years to come. But given the region's award-winning earthquake performances, such confidence may have been misplaced. In 1991 there would come even greater testament to the questionable engineering that Geddes had in store for Windy Craggy: That winter, heavy snows would crush six of the seven buildings it had designed and erected at the mine site, along with the mine portal and part of the access road. This did little to instill confidence in the company's ability to build earthquakeproof reservoirs in the most seismically active region on earth.

From camp that evening at the meeting place of the Tat and Alsek Rivers, Careless and the group watched the grassy uplands above. The lush green hills were bursting with forget-me-nots, mountain buttercups, wild geraniums, and paintbrush. Dall sheep and mountain goats grazed high, out of the way of the grizzlies. Ric asked himself how anyone could do what Geddes was intent on doing to this elegant, eloquent landscape. The answer, he determined, lay in perspective, and Geddes's was one of greed.

On the flight home he made his calculations. Geddes had already spent $50 million exploring Windy Craggy, and in the process had gouged the mountain with a 13,000-foot mine shaft. It had built its mine camp and surveyed an access road. Already it had applied to the B.C. government for permission to proceed. By the time Careless was back in the office, his sources were telling him he'd never stop the momentum of this mining magnate. But Careless wasn't about to give up—nor was his partner in life and in activism, Dona Reel, who had immediately committed to helping him save the river. Nor was Johnny Mikes.

With time ticking against the Tat, Careless decided to go straight for the jugular. Knowing that roads were arteries through which all other menaces to wilderness flowed, he and Mikes researched the company's road claim. One immediate concern was a recent onslaught of all-terrain vehicles carrying bear and wolf poachers. Joyously, the two advocates discovered that Geddes had slashed its survey line without a permit. They held the violation up for the Canadian ministers to see; the officials immediately halted the road's progress.

It bought the Tat some much-needed time.

With lightning speed Careless, Reel, and Mikes set up a non-profit organization called Tatshenshini Wild. Within a few weeks, they lured two young, wide-eyed, and eager volunteers to work with them. Next they began sending out press releases to media everywhere. Their motto was, "Tatshenshini: Protect North America's Wildest River." Soon *Tatshenshini*, as thorny as it was to pronounce, was rolling off the tongues of British Columbians across the province. Public meetings and slide shows were organized and played to standing-room-only crowds.

Crossing the Border

Meanwhile, Tatshenshini Wild's investigative efforts were paying off, too. The group learned that Geddes was going to need a U.S. port in which to deliver its slurry; the U.S. government and voters might object to this if they knew what was at stake and how little environmental assessment had been done on the Canadian end.

There were several reasons for a possible U.S. veto: First, in the event of a pipeline rupture, fish kills would jeopardize the Chilkat Eagle Preserve north of Haines, Alaska, where the world's largest population of bald eagles lived. Second, dewatering of the pipeline, at 360,000 gallons a day, would put many fisheries at risk—especially the Lynn Canal, which by itself brought in $41 million a year to the Alaskan economy and provided hundreds of jobs.

The Windy Craggy mine would also violate four international treaties—the U.S.–Canada Boundary Waters Treaty, the Pacific Salmon Treaty, and the Migratory Birds Convention were the first three. After the United Nations named Glacier Bay National Park a World Heritage Site—the highest form of international recognition of land for "outstanding universal value to mankind"—Canada signed the fourth treaty, the World Heritage Convention. By signing this, Canada was obligated not to take any deliberate measure which might damage directly or indirectly the "natural heritage" of the Site.

This was great news. If the United States opposed the mine, Canada would be more inclined to follow its lead. But this made for difficult grassroots campaigning: Never before had there been a transcontinental wilderness campaign. It meant travel and time for lobbying—not only to the Canadian federal government but also to those of the Yukon, B.C., and Alaska. It also meant time in Washington, D.C. It was a lot for a small group of citizens to take on—especially in pre-Internet times.

Careless contacted Brock Evans, an American wilderness activist who had become vice president of the Audubon Society. After hearing the story of the Tatshenshini, Evans agreed to send a letter to Geddes on behalf of the American conservation community. The letter was then made public by the Canadian Sierra Club during Geddes's annual shareholders meeting in Toronto. Geddes had been exposed, and the campaign began to take on a life of its own.

Tatshenshini Wild's grassroots efforts caught the attention of both Canada's and America's heavy-hitting conservation groups—

An ice wall along the Tat.

groups like The Wilderness Society, the National Wildlife Federation, American Wildlands, the World Wildlife Fund, the Canadian Nature Federation, and the Canadian Parks and Wilderness Society. Now the small group could get some leverage. But the big guns were all so embroiled in other issues that this relatively obscure one didn't register at the top of their charts. Careless realized then that he would have to do with people of influence what Mikes had done with him: Get their asses onto the river.

Pitching the River

Careless and Mikes pitched the plight of the Tat to sixteen commercial outfitters, who agreed to donate river trips to the cause. After all, if Geddes completed its wilderness open-heart surgery, the outfitters would be out of business on the Tat. Nevertheless, it was generous of the companies—mostly mom-and-pop concerns without a fat profit margin. Following extensive rounds of cold calls, Careless, Reel, and Mikes found that they had managed to book the best—photographers and writers from *National Geographic, Outside, Life,* and *Equinox* had all signed up. Journalists from North America's best newspapers snagged spots. Dozens of top conservationists came along as well.

In June 1990, after only six months of campaigning, the key folks were on the river. The Tatshenshini did the rest of the job, selling itself as the spectacular wilderness that it was. But the game wasn't entirely being played by bigwig politicians and media representatives; there was still a need for the grassroots to grow, and there was room for a river rat to make a splash.

Like Johnny Mikes before him, boater Ken Madsen was searching for a way to help save the river. As one of Canada's top paddlers, Madsen decided to organize a paddling expedition unparalleled in its scope. Tatshenshini Wilderness Quest would be an effort to paddle all the rivers at risk from the Windy Craggy project: the Tat, the Alsek, and the Chilkat (along which the pipeline would run to Haines). Following this journey, Madsen vowed, he would author a book about the region and his experiences paddling its rivers. He also committed to producing a slide show of the journey, which he would then take on tour across Canada.

The trip was a daunting one. In the twenty years since Blackadar's sub-marine ride, only three other groups had successfully kayaked the Tat-Alsek's Turnback Canyon. Madsen and his team pulled it off with moxie. But it wasn't the danger of Turnback that stayed with Madsen; about the river he wrote, "You don't need to be submerged in a violent rapid to feel this land's magic . . . wherever I travel in this wilderness, I feel a sense of insignificance, a sense that I don't have power over the landscape. It's a good feeling."

Mission accomplished, Madsen returned to publish his book, named for the expedition, and then took to the road to share his experiences with fellow boaters and other Canadians.

Broadening the Base

By 1991, Careless felt the issue had received enough recognition that he could take it to the next level. He organized a conference to which he invited the best and the brightest wilderness warriors from Sitka to San Diego—and of course from D.C. Tatshenshini International (TI) was born, an alchemic union of fifty environmental groups that collectively represented more than ten million North American citizens.

Tatshenshini Wild was a volunteer effort, and revenue came in at a trickle. The groups in Tatshenshini International all supported themselves, but the task of communicating with each of them, as well as with the public and media of two large nations, was a problem for the small central organization. Tat Wild had a dinosaur of a computer and no fax machine or copier. And what foundation would fund an unknown group with a little-known cause that bled across national borders? Few were interested. Then a Tatshenshini Wild board member—the well-known B.C. climber and outdoor equipment wholesaler Michael Dunn—sutured together a proposal for the Outdoor Industry Conservation Alliance (OICA). The result literally guaranteed the success of the campaign.

From the Alliance the river group requested $29,628 to purchase a desktop publishing system and produce a poster and educational video. The Conservation Alliance understood immediately the far-reaching consequences of the proposed mine and the significant role that Tatshenshini Wild was playing in stopping it. The Alliance funded the request in full, and within weeks of depositing the check in the bank, Tatshenshini Wild had produced top-notch science reports and media kits. Outdoor photographer Art Wolfe donated a stunning image of the river, which was converted into a poster. The image was distributed widely and fixed the river in the mind's eye of the public. The poster was sold at slide shows and events, producing another much-needed $12,000 in income for the group. The video was a hit, too; because of the logistics involved in getting to the Tatshenshini, a great number of news reporters had been unable to cover the story. With the new press kit and video footage, however, the plight of the river and all it sustained was now being shown on news stations across the continent. The Conservation Alliance grant was the crucial donation that the campaign received—especially at this key stage—and it was money well spent.

Tatshenshini Wild and its coalition arm, Tatshenshini International, were now running at full throttle. TI's collaborative operations were remarkably fluid and effective—most coalitions get bogged down in process and diluted by consensus. Careless described TI as a fully functioning ecosystem, much like that of the river region itself. TI operated without a central hierarchy, instead urging each group to create and work its own niche. The original Tatshenshini Wild served as the epicenter of communication, and in the years predating the World Wide Web, this role was arduous. Nevertheless, things ran gracefully as each group took off running with its part in the process. In one fine example of ecosystem spirit, American Rivers, the leading river advocacy group in the United States, put the Tatshenshini on its Ten Most Endangered Rivers list—the first time a Canadian waterway had ever been listed. By 1992 the Tat had moved up to the number two spot on the list, forcing Washington and the Canadian government to take real notice.

Getting Political

Soon key political figures were on the rafts and headed down the river—prominent individuals like Canada's former prime minister Pierre Trudeau, the Canadian minister of finance and the B.C. minister of the environment, and Katie McGinty, then an aide to Senator Al Gore. McGinty was so taken with the Tat that she returned to D.C. and urged her boss to get involved. On April 8 Senator Gore delivered a Senate resolution opposing the proposed mine, and at an American Rivers press conference he made the statement, "The development of a huge open-pit copper mine in the midst of one of the world's most pristine regions is an environmental nightmare that threatens the river and every living thing in the region." It was uncharacteristically definitive from a politician.

Gore persuaded Congressman Wayne Owens from Utah to sponsor the same legislative action on the House side. Careless flew down to testify before the House Interior Committee, along with another lead Alaskan environmentalist, Peter Enticknap, and Native Tinglit Caroline Powell. Powell's words swept like a chilling glacial wind across the committee chamber's floor. Reflecting the concerns of her people, who depended upon the Tat's salmon runs for their survival, she stated, "Windy Craggy's proposed man-made lake . . . is an imminent lake of genocide to the Yakutat Tinglit people of the gulf coast of Alaska." Careless's words also resonated. He articulated House Joint Resolution 460's goals: to simultaneously stop the Geddes mine and protect the Tat forever from future encroachments. Such protection would connect the adjoining national parks in Alaska and the Yukon; together the lands would total 23 million acres—the largest contiguously protected area in North America. Looking to the United States to set the environmental standard for the project, Careless concluded with a moving synopsis:

> We believe that the United States has so much to gain through the preservation of Tatshenshini and the completion of the largest international wilderness reserve in the world. Crucial U.S. National Park, wildlife and fisheries values would be safeguarded. And by working with Canada, together our two nations would create a global showpiece of transboundary environmental cooperation. What a superlative legacy to bestow upon the world and future generations.

The grassroots campaign rattled and hummed across the continent. Meanwhile, the political outlook took a surprising turn for the better. Al Gore became vice president, and Katie McGinty joined him in the White House as the administration's top environmental adviser. And for the first time in thirty years, the government of British Columbia had a green side to it. The new premier, Mike Harcourt, had heard plenty about the Tat. As soon as he took office, he ordered a review of the Tatshenshini situation; the report confirmed that "massive and perpetual toxic pollution was likely to occur if the mine proceeded."

But Geddes and the all-powerful mining industry continued to pump millions into lobbying efforts to counteract the burgeoning

Dona Reel and Ric Careless.

opposition to Windy Craggy. Their lawyers and specialists visited government officials continentwide, arguing that this opposition spelled the end of mining for all British Columbia, if not North America. Ultimately the mining advocates faced off with the tree huggers and river runners over the desk of Anne Edwards, British Columbia's minister of mining. Even in its final moments, as the B.C. cabinet debated the final decision, the campaign pulsated with intensity.

The Pulse Prevails

But as Careless writes, "From a moral standpoint, the force was with us." In June 1993 Premier Harcourt announced that the Windy Craggy mine was a flat blue line on the screen—by declaring all 2.4 million acres of the Tatshenshini region a provincial wilderness park. In a public speech Harcourt said:

> *This million-hectare park, which is twice the size of the Grand Canyon, will ensure the permanent protection of an area internationally recognized for its unique wildlife, biodiversity, and wilderness recreation values.*

> *It will protect one of the last strongholds of North America's grizzly bear population, protect the rare glacier bear, and sustain the Tatshenshini-Alsek as one of the three major salmon-bearing rivers on the northern Pacific coast.*

> *This is one of the most spectacular wilderness areas in the world, and today British Columbia is living up to its global responsibility to keep it that way.*

It was the first day of summer and the precise date that Tatshenshini Wild had chosen years before as its target for sending the mine to its grave.

A year and a half later, the Tatshenshini received its United Nations designation as a World Heritage Site, and it will forever remain the healthy heart of twenty-three million acres of St. Elias wilderness in Alaska, the Yukon, and British Columbia. The Tat is now recognized as the only free-flowing river in British Columbia to be protected in its entirety—from its headwaters to its merging with the sea.

In celebration Ric Careless and Dona Reel took their two children on a raft down the Tatshenshini. It was a small group, a reunion of friends and family coming together to rejoice with the river. Sitting again at the confluence, where the Tat and Alsek join forces, Careless remembered having been there only a few years before and making the pledge. He sat in silence, feeling the pulse of the place, its waters, its mountains, its ice fields, its bears and birds and fish. It was the same pulse he had felt among the fifty groups of Tatshenshini International, its ten million supporters, its convergence of politicians and river rats. It was the pulse of life itself.

BIBLIOGRAPHY

Blackadar, Walt. "Caught up in a Hell of Whitewater." *Sports Illustrated*, 1972.

Careless, Ric. *To Save the Wild Earth: Field Notes from the Environmental Front Line*. Vancouver: Raincoast Books, 1997; Seattle: The Mountaineers, 1997.

Madsen, Ken. *Tatshenshini, Wilderness Quest: and Other River Adventures*. Canada: Western Canada Wilderness Committee and Primrose Publishing, 1991.

Rauber, Paul. "No River Wilder." *Sierra*, January/February 1993.

Searle, Rick. "Journey to the Ice Age." *Equinox* 55 (January/February 1991): 24–35.

Subcommittee on National Parks and Public Lands, House Committee on Interior and Insular Affairs. "Testimony of Ric Careless, Executive Director, Tatshenshini Wild." Washington, D.C., 1992. Photocopy.

Summer Wild Productions. *Tatshenshini River Wild*. Englewood, Colo.: Westcliffe Publishers, 1993.

Tatshenshini Wild. *Conservation Alliance Tatshenshini Wild Funding Proposal*. Vancouver: Tatshenshini Wild, 1991.

———. *Tatshenshini-Alsek: North America's Wildest River Briefing Document*. Vancouver: Tatshenshini Wild, 1993.

Art of Stone

New York State's Shawangunks
1991–1993

"Gothic—of or relating to an art style flourishing especially in northern Europe from the 12th through the 19th centuries and distinguished by an austere verticality and a tendency toward naturalism."

—*Webster's Third New International Dictionary*

The young man had immigrated from Dresden before the war. Now he was perched on a rock above New York State's Hudson River, astonished at the untouched natural landscapes of this New World around him. It was much like his homeland had been—before the Old World deconstructed its own open spaces. The year was 1935. He had just completed the first ascent of the luminous white rock on Shawangunk Ridge. He named his route the Gargoyle.

The immigrant's name was Fritz Wiessner, and he knew stone. In Dresden he had crafted what were the most difficult rock climbs in the world at the time. From his quartz vantage point that day, he could see miles of rolling ridgetops crowned with spare vertical escarpments. They made graceful arcs, like flying buttresses on a medieval cathedral. These steep, clean cliffs were some of the best he'd ever seen.

What Fritz couldn't see then was the future of these crags. In less than fifty years, these quiet, bucolic hinterlands would be overcast by a shadow—the New World's credo of progress, profit, and growth. Real estate developers and scores of urbanites seeking

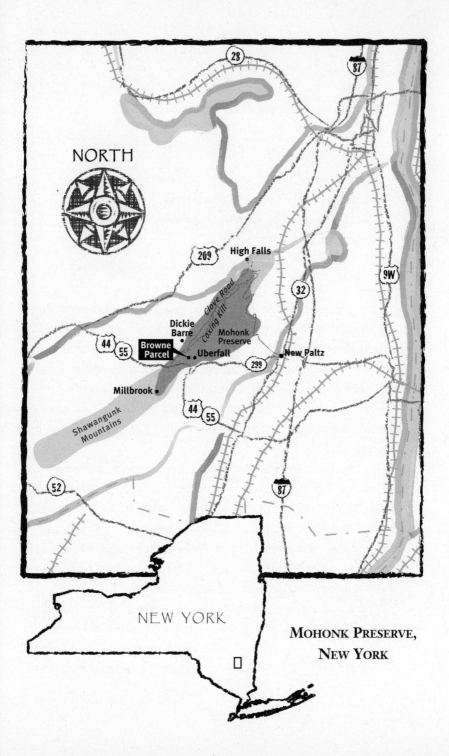

NORTH

28

87

209   High Falls

Clove Road

32

9W

Dickie
Barre

Coxing Kill

Mohonk
Preserve

44
55

Browne
Parcel   Uberfall

New Paltz

299

Millbrook

44
55

*Shawangunk
Mountains*

52

87

NEW YORK

MOHONK PRESERVE,
NEW YORK

escape from New York City's mad hustle would flock to this place like bats to a cave at sunrise. The stone faces on which Fritz climbed would become fortresses—the area's only natural defense in a battle against campgrounds and cars, as realtors looked for a way to access the untouched, scenic views that waited above them.

But to develop the ridgetops would have been a desecration. By 1980 these hilltops would cradle the last dwarf pines in the world—one of the few remaining ancient forests in North America. Among them and on the adjacent talus slopes lay archaic plant communities and twenty-seven rare or endangered plants and animals, all relics from an earlier time in desperate need of preservation.

Nor could Fritz see that it would be climbers like himself who would hold up the figurative cross in the face of the New World vampires.

Modern Times in the Gunks

Time passed on and so did Fritz Wiessner. It was 1991 and, like his predecessor, John Juraschek knew stone. But JJ wasn't climbing as much as he would have liked; now that he'd taken on the role of executive director of The Access Fund, he was instead beating the bushes for money to help protect climbing areas. JJ's new position embodied the irony of all environmental activist jobs: not a lot of pay and an overload of work that kept you in the office instead of out in the places that you loved. It was a tough task, especially since the young group hadn't yet gained any stature. "In those early days people still thought of us as the 'California Bolting Fund,'" JJ recalls. "No one took us seriously as resource advocates." The office had taken over the tiny two-bedroom southern California home that JJ and his wife shared. He worked for peanuts; she volunteered hours of her time.

The Shawangunks were definitely not a place for a bolting group. By the late 1980s, while hot spots of American climbing enjoyed prefixed, machine-bolted routes and permanent protection, the Shawangunks would remain a bastion of old-style climbing.

Both community consensus and the law decreed that climbers use removable gear—like hexes and stoppers—to ascend. Traditional tools. Tools that Fritz Wiessner would have used.

But JJ was a real advocate for "the Gunks"—as they had been called by local residents and visiting climbers since Fritz Wiessner's glory days. The term described the northern end of a ridge system that stretched 50 miles from the New Jersey border up into New York, where it shored up the Catskill Mountains. JJ had fallen in love with the Gunks early on in his climbing career in a nerve-racking but ultimately successful ascent of Shockley's Ceiling, a classic exposed 5.5 roof problem. He was a bit rattled before he even began the climb—since his partner, while belaying JJ up the first pitch, had just managed to grab the end of the rope as it came undone from his diaper harness. It was a day JJ never forgot.

Since then he had been drawn to the escarpment's uplifted architecture, designed by the earth's own folding and faulting. He found the vales and forests between the ridges lush and idyllic in a European sort of way. The few human edifices that dotted the landscape revealed Old World influence, too—especially the old castle hotel near Mohonk Lake, whose grounds featured dirt carriage paths rather than paved streets. Indeed, the Gunks were old—and they had hardly changed since the Ice Age that masoned their stone relief.

Then JJ heard about something that threatened to alter the face of the Gunks forever. A privately owned chunk of land was about to hit the real estate market, and excitement among developers was running high. The cliffs on the property held some of the Gunks' finer rock climbs—routes like the Main Line, Eowyn, and Muriel's Nose. The beloved Millbrook Ridge Trail traversed the clifftop. JJ realized that any enterprising new landowners would likely eliminate access to the trail and climbing routes in order to limit their potential liability. That was how the New World worked.

Access or Excess?

Alarmed, the young executive director did some homework. The property was called the Browne Parcel, after its seller, George Browne. It extended from the road all the way up to the ridgetop, and it had recently been zoned for commercial development. Located in the Near Trapps area, the parcel was only twenty-five acres in size but held one of the three natural cols, or breaks, on the entire ridge. It also housed a natural spring that bubbled out of the dark recesses of a stone cavern. There was talk of the parcel being sold to a developer who would use the col, known as Smede's Cove, to access the top of the Eastern Escarpment and establish a large commercial campground. There were also rumors of access being sold to utility companies, which wanted to use the col as a shortcut route for power, phone, and sewage lines. The local Mohonk Preserve already owned the land containing the other two cols, so the Browne Parcel was the last remaining potential gateway to the ecosystem on top. As a climber who had cut his teeth in the Gunks, this land sale and the threats it posed distressed JJ more than any other issue that The Access Fund had ever looked at.

Normally the Mohonk Preserve would have immediately bought up such a property—it had done so with many other parcels in the area. But the listing was ill-timed for the largest privately owned nature preserve in New York State. Although Mohonk was well established and had money to spend, purchasing the parcel would have jeopardized resources committed to other important acquisitions already in progress that year. One such property included a cliff that a developer wanted to blast and then use as a site for his home. Surrounded by preserve lands, the structure would have seemed an eyesore to many people. Caught between a rock and a hard place, the preserve seemed unlikely to be of much help.

The situation was causing JJ to lose sleep. Could a small, scrappy group raise enough money for such a purchase? The fund had never undertaken such a large project. It was barely paying its bills; most of its work to protect America's climbing areas consisted of trail cleanups. JJ really wished that the preserve would just get out there and raise the extra money for the acquisition.

The Smiley Legacy

After all, the Mohonk Preserve was legendary for its property purchases and environmental stewardship. It was in keeping with a family legacy; in 1869 Quaker philanthropists and twin brothers Albert and Alfred Smiley had purchased nearby Mohonk Lake. On its shores they established Mohonk Mountain House, a hotel that looked more like a fantastical Bavarian citadel than the resort they had dedicated to contemplating nature as a means for spiritual growth. Over the years, in keeping with their regard for the natural world, the Smiley family acquired an estate of 7,500 surrounding acres. By the early 1960s the Mohonk Trust was in business, becoming the Mohonk Preserve in 1978. Over the course of its existence, the preserve had purchased many properties similar to the Browne Parcel. Its first acquisition was the Trapps area, a 487-acre tract possessing uniquely gorgeous geological features and rich with flora and fauna. Even at that early date, the Trapps Parcel was known to contain some of the most prominent rock climbing in the United States—second only to the granite walls of California's Yosemite Valley. It was clear why JJ and other climbers were so concerned about the future of the Gunks.

One family member in particular had given the preserve the philosophical scaffolding on which it now stood. After forty years of Mountain House management, Daniel Smiley threw himself into what was to be his true calling. A largely self-taught naturalist, he went on to manage the Mohonk Preserve on two principles: First, conservation is a moral obligation; humans' relationship with nature should be governed by ethics. Second, "understanding is requisite to a durable accommodation between human interests and the natural environment."

The Trapps Parcel contains some of the most prominent rock climbing in the United States.

To be sure, Smiley walked his two-pronged talk and made enormous contributions along the way. On 16,000 note cards, he had recorded observations of weather and species that turned out to be priceless to the natural science community. In 1931 he documented the initial appearance of acid rain in Shawangunk lakes; his thirty-year database of pH levels in precipitation allowed the preserve to play a key role in the issue. Smiley noted, too, that as early as 1910 the wild turkey was nearly extinct in the region. In 1970 he partnered with Cornell University to release captive-bred peregrine falcon chicks into the wild.

Thanks to the vision of the Smiley clan, the Mohonk Preserve fast became a model in private land conservation, and it now moors the collection of land acquisitions and easements that make up the broader Shawangunk Natural Area. So spectacular and ecologically significant is the region that it was named one of the world's Last Great Places by The Nature Conservancy. Currently the preserve acts as a sentinel for a body of land about the size of Manhattan—which is located just two hours away and holds more than twenty million people.

Population Vs. Preservation

By the 1990s many of these people seemed to have found their way to the Gunks' Mohonk Preserve. Climbers made up a good portion of the 100,000 now visiting each year; like modern-day gargoyles, their bodies seemed to decorate every square inch of rock face. And there were thousands of cyclists, hikers, and bird-watchers, too, each seeking refuge in the sanctuary of the Gunks' hills. It was clear to John Juraschek that the Gunks were being loved to death. Although the low-impact recreationists meant well, the sheer number of them was a problem that had to be addressed, along with the impending threat of development.

Many nature preserves prohibit recreation within their boundaries altogether for fear of disruption to natural processes. But the

Smileys had believed that land stewardship was a multifaceted concept centered not only on studying and safeguarding natural communities but on maintaining the historical uses of a place, too. To inspire people to connect with the natural world in a meaningful way, the Mohonk Preserve decided early on to allow low-impact, contemplative recreation and other appropriate activities, such as environmental education classes. Over the years its staff had ensured that sensitive areas and species remained undisturbed, but everyone wondered if they could manage the 1990s numbers of climbers and hikers. The parking lots and trails were oversaturated, and many visitors didn't understand the delicate nature of the ground—or rocks—upon which they trod. Many took their privileges for granted.

Others did not. Local climber Russ Clune joined the boards of both the Mohonk Preserve and The Access Fund to help support their missions—both of which he believed in devoutly. An accomplished climber, Clune had been climbing in the Gunks since 1977. He still remembers waking up that first morning in the camping area and seeing the white cliffs: "I'd been climbing then for only a short time but I was hooked for good. I instantly loved the place and couldn't believe that I'd been raised a scant 75 miles to the south but never knew it existed. I feel incredibly fortunate to be one of those people who finds his soul's home and knows it." Given this conviction, Clune has served as an excellent conduit between the climbing community and the preserve. He tries to convey to climbers how important the preserve is, and how generous is its recreation policy. "I can think of few other privately owned areas that offer as much freedom," he says.

Such freedom is not to be taken lightly, because recreation wasn't always so welcome at Mohonk. Following the first climbing fatality in 1959, the Smileys considered shutting down access to the cliffs. Out of touch with contemporary climbing culture and practices, the Appalachian Mountain Club (AMC) stepped in as a poorly suited mediator, proposing a complicated certification system to "qualify" climbers to lead routes. The "Appies" patrolled the cliff bands, ordering the uncertified to descend from the cliffs.

The AMC's Big Brother attitude flew in the face of everything Gunks climbers—all nonconforming hedonists—embraced. The climbing community responded with vertical displays of rebellion—like climbing naked in front of tourists and urinating off a local pub's roof onto customers' heads. The AMC backed off in exasperation, and the Smileys left the cliffs open. By the 1980s more than 1,000 routes were listed on the three most popular cliffs, and climbers were policing themselves rigorously.

Beyond Climbing

If the Browne Parcel were developed and access to the cliffs restricted, would climbers resort to the acts of defiance they had used last time they felt their access threatened? Hopefully not. Mostly, though, JJ was concerned about the ecology of the ridge. He knew there were more than 200 species of nesting birds in addition to spotted salamanders, black bears, bobcats, and foxes— all creatures incompatible with New World sprawl. He also knew that the lower talus system of the Browne Parcel contained a very endangered plant species called Bradley's spleenwort. Of the 31,500 acres that make up the northern Shawangunks, only 58 percent was permanently protected from development through land acquisitions and conservation easements. The fate of a strategically located property like the Browne Parcel would indeed affect the future of the Gunks' ecosystems.

JJ took the leap. "We have to get involved," he said to his colleagues at The Access Fund. "Even if we find that climbing is incompatible with protecting the resources we're setting out to protect, it is still the right thing to do." Now he had to convince other climbers that this was an effort worth taking on.

But first JJ contacted of Friends of the Shawangunks, a small advocacy group for the region. Together with the Mohonk

Preserve and the Open Space Institute of New York, Friends of the Gunks had begun negotiations with landowner George Browne. JJ learned that through the pro bono legal services of Bob Anderberg, the director of the Open Space Institute, the groups were already orchestrating an option to buy as well as devising a strategy to subdivide the property in the hope of eliminating its commercial zoning status. When these tasks were accomplished, the property would be something the Mohonk Preserve could acquire—if the money to complete the deal could be found.

Next JJ got on the horn with local Access Fund contact Dave Rosenstein and asked that he check out ways they could help with the purchase. Rosenstein, like everyone else in the climbing community, knew that the Gunks housed one of the most revered and historic climbing areas in the nation—if not the world. The Gunks had weaned the greats—like Lynn Hill. She was the first and remains the only climber to have free-climbed the Nose on the Yosemite Valley's El Capitan wall in a single day. Rosenstein immediately understood the significance of acquiring this property. Without another thought, he and JJ pledged to the other groups that they would help raise the money. Together with Friends of the Shawangunks, they signed an option to buy on December 1, 1992. If they couldn't complete the deal in twelve months, an ancient world could be entombed in a modern-day sarcophagus of trailer pads.

Together the groups searched religiously for donors to help with the acquisition. Unfortunately, many reliable sources had already been tapped for other projects—it was late in the fiscal year. But there was good news amid the dark musings: During the course of the land survey, an additional fifteen acres were discovered—somehow they had been missed in a prior survey. Seven hundred feet of cliff and talus were part of the late discovery. This was potentially a very significant bonus for climbers and a definite plus for creepers—like the imperiled Bradley's spleenwort—which needed such habitat. The parcel also included long-established hiking trails along the ridgetop and at the base of the cliffs.

Following JJ's lead, The Access Fund had adopted a generous vision for the Browne Parcel. Once the parcel belonged to the preserve, there was no guarantee that climbing privileges would continue if the habitat were deemed too fragile for human intrusion. Juraschek recalls explaining this to other climbers: "Going into the purchase we are very clear that while there are a few classic routes on the property, really we aren't doing this so much for climbing as for the sheer act of preserving the overall resource that the Mohonk Ridge represents."

This statement marked a real shift in the climbing community's consciousness—and the efforts of The Access Fund. Everyone was thinking bigger: thinking about the needs of the ecosystem surrounding the cliffs, and the larger amounts of money that would be required to protect them.

Gambling on a Young Group

But JJ was getting nervous. He was running out of sources to tap for the purchase. Then he had an epiphany. He called Kathleen Beamer at REI, who served on the board of the Outdoor Industry Conservation Alliance (OICA). Would the Alliance be interested in funding such a thing? Beamer said it very well might be. So in record time JJ crafted a proposal for the land acquisition, requesting the entire sum of $30,300 to purchase the property on behalf of the Mohonk Preserve and Friends of the Shawangunks. Next he called Libby Ellis, who represented Patagonia on the OICA board at the time. He lobbied her intensely, and although Ellis was initially unsure about funding such a young group with no track record, she became convinced that it was an ideal project for the Alliance. "In our discussions JJ was so passionate about saving the Gunks. And I was impressed with the collaboration they had initiated with the other groups. I really developed great faith in The Access Fund during that time."

Juraschek didn't stop there. Through personal notes, he aggressively lobbied the Conservation Alliance's members. In a heartfelt plea he wrote:

> *To finally bring this project to the brink of fruition has been no small accomplishment and has involved many, many people and organizations, all with the single realization that this project represents a special and extremely urgent opportunity for preservation. . . .*
>
> *Placing this property under the rightful stewardship of the Mohonk Preserve will guarantee once and for all that commercial development will never be allowed to intrude into an area that has come to occupy a special place in the hearts of thousands of people.*
>
> *When you sit down to vote on this latest round of proposals, I know you will agree with me that this project surpasses all of the Coalition's [sic] aims and is more than worthy of funding.*

The Conservation Alliance met that winter during the Outdoor Retailer trade show to discuss funding proposals. Its members were very impressed with The Access Fund's request for support. But they were committed to funding projects that generally had more of a grassroots activism dimension; this outright land purchase seemed a bit outside their box. Ellis and Beamer, who in their daily work supporting environmental groups on behalf of Patagonia and REI understood intimately the issues and threats that faced the natural world, said that this was one purchase the Alliance should consider. The Gunks were internationally significant—both as a climbing destination and as an ecosystem. This project, they reasoned, was a perfect fit for the Alliance.

Sam Davidson, policy analyst for The Access Fund, remembers hanging out with JJ during the trade show. "We were awaiting the results of the Alliance's decision, and JJ was chewing his knuckles and pacing around, he wanted it so bad." Davidson, a tall, composed attorney from southern California, tethered JJ during the stress of it all but hands nearly all the credit for the effort to Juraschek. "JJ's a classic Type-A character, and all of the theatrics and stress and urgency of his work style were brought to bear on this project. He, more than any other, was responsible for the whole thing coming together."

John Juraschek (fourth from the left) and Dave Rosenstein (far right) present a check to the Mohonk Preserve staff.

And come together it did. The board voted to fund the project in its entirety, effectively driving a stake through the heart of Shawangunk development.

The Browne Parcel was bought; the area remained unscathed. But the good work didn't stop there. The Conservation Alliance's contribution not only allowed the Mohonk Preserve to move ahead with its other important land acquisitions but also freed up other Access Fund money, $7,000 of which it donated to climber education and conservation efforts at the preserve. It also provided $5,000 to construct a much-needed connector trail from the parking lot to the crags along the Undercliff Carriage Road. The trail diverted hikers and climbers around fragile habitat and provided a safe route into the preserve. With this, much of the pressure put on the preserve by increasing numbers of visitors was relieved.

That June The Access Fund, the Mohonk Preserve, Friends of the Shawangunks, and the Open Space Institute of New York met with local residents and outdoor enthusiasts to celebrate their successes. To the preserve staff, Dave Rosenstein and John Juraschek handed over an imitation check of gothic proportions. No one could miss the five-figure number on its sum line. That same day a plaque was dedicated to climbing legend Fritz Wiessner and his partner Hans Kraus for their cultural and architectural contributions to Gunks' climbing. Fritz had passed away only a few years before, but his lore lived on. Through the course of the day, people reminisced about Fritz's impressive moonlight ascents of Gunks' classics—which he continued well into his eighties. Among the eulogizers was Kraus, who had recently been diagnosed with the prostate cancer that would kill him in a year's time, his body shrinking from the solid formation it had once been. He reminded climbers that the advent of sticky shoes, climbing gyms, and high-tech equipment may have helped them ascend much more difficult routes than he or Fritz ever could, but in the process he hoped they hadn't lost sight of the true meaning of climbing in the Gunks and within the Mohonk Preserve—as a communication with the self and with nature.

As for The Access Fund, the faith that the Conservation Alliance placed in the fund's vision put the group on the map—giving it stature with land managers, climbers, and private property owners across the country. JJ is grateful: "For those of us who have come to know and love the wild places of America, and have come to earn our living in an industry that profits from a very precious and finite resource, the Conservation Alliance is the single best thing in the outdoor industry."

Hans Kraus speaks about his legendary climbing partner Fritz Wiessner and their days in the Shawangunks.

But it wasn't just climbers and conservationists who celebrated the purchase of the Browne Parcel and the ultimate preservation of the Shawangunk Eastern Escarpment in its entirety. A charming letter appeared in *Ridgelines*, the newsletter of Friends of the Shawangunks. It read, "I look up and there it is—beautiful now as in the past. And with your efforts, the Shawangunks should be inspiring for generations to come. . . ."

The letter was signed by a farmer who for forty years had lived and tended crops at the foot of the Gunks.

There was a time when Europe disavowed its elegant gothic cathedrals—even Chartres and Notre Dame. Many places of worship were destroyed in an effort to modernize—in the name of progress. We now understand the shortsightedness of eliminating such ancient treasures, such works of art. Once gone, they cannot be replaced. Author and naturalist Terry Tempest Williams wrote, "Just as we designate art, we designate wilderness." Now the Shawangunks are rightfully both—for generations to come.

BIBLIOGRAPHY

The Access Fund. *Proposal to the Outdoor Industry Conservation Alliance.* New Paltz, N.Y.: The Access Fund, 1992.

The Mohonk Preserve. *Realizing the Vision: A Case for Support.* New Paltz, N.Y.: The Mohonk Preserve, 1996.

————. *Ridgelines* 111, 113, and 115. New Paltz, N.Y.: The Mohonk Preserve, 1997–98.

Roberts, David. "High Adventures in the Gunks." *Smithsonian,* August 1996, 30–41.

Williams, Terry Tempest. *Leap.* New York: Pantheon Books, 2000.

Blood Roots

InterTribal Sinkyone Wilderness Park, California
1986–1997

In the distance there are two red dots—one large, one small, both bright as poppies. The dots move along the forested road; the camera fixes on them as they approach. The larger spot crystallizes into a man in a bright red T-shirt, a Native American man. Watching over his shoulder for approaching cars, he jogs slowly enough to pace the footsteps of the small Indian child, who wears a similar red shirt, running next to him. The camera trains on them as they run by. The four-year-old clutches in his small fist a sacred eagle staff, which he'll pass off to another child down the road.

This is one leg of a 100-mile relay run along northern California's Highway 101, from Coyote Valley to Sinkyone Wilderness State Park. Youths from a dozen northern California tribes are participating; their goal is to draw attention to the land surrounding them—their ancestral land. A land whose primeval redwood forest is coveted by logging corporations. A land that has been torn from beneath the feet of the Sinkyone people.

Once part of a much-vaster redwood rain forest, the Sinkyone has been ravaged by more than three decades of clear-cuts. And the people with historic roots in this soil were nearly annihilated in a holocaust carried out by white settlers during the 1850s. The message of this run, this passing of the culture from one person to another, is one of remembering, and of traditional Indian stewardship. Only when the Native People can reconnect with and heal their land will they be healed, too.

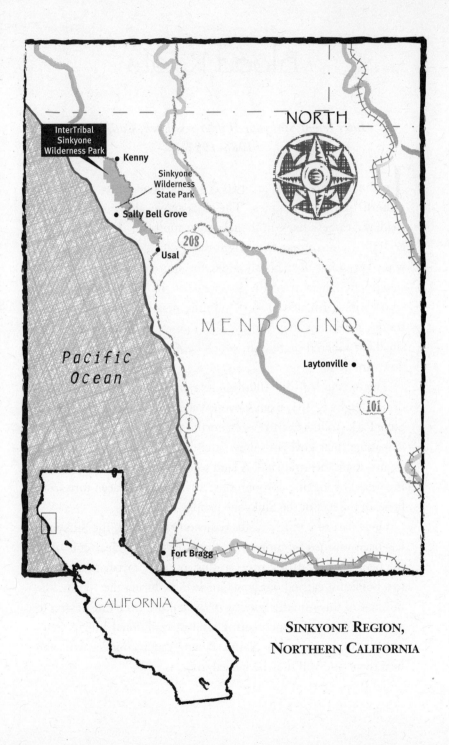

NORTH

InterTribal
Sinkyone
Wilderness Park

• Kenny

Sinkyone
Wilderness
State Park

• Sally Bell Grove

208

• Usal

MENDOCINO

Pacific
Ocean

Laytonville •

101

1

• Fort Bragg

CALIFORNIA

SINKYONE REGION,
NORTHERN CALIFORNIA

Highlights of the 1991 run were documented on celluloid as part of *The Run to Save Sinkyone*, a film written and directed by Jonathan Rosales, a Chiricahua Apache. He was sixty-one years old when he made this, his first film, a documentary so moving that in 1995 it was selected for screening at Robert Redford's internationally acclaimed Sundance Film Festival held in Park City, Utah.

It wasn't meant to be that kind of film. It had originally been produced as a fund-raising and educational tool for the InterTribal Sinkyone Wilderness Council, a consortium of eleven federally recognized California tribes, including the Yuki, Pomo, and Wailaki, so they could buy back and restore the land that had once been their home.

Each of these tribes has cultural and historical roots at Sinkyone, which lies in the northwestern portion of Mendocino County, 200 miles north of San Francisco. Part of the "Lost Coast," the steep, verdant slopes fall abruptly from redwood forest into foaming surf. For thousands of years the earthly gifts of the Sinkyone area supported one of North America's largest populations of Native People.

Today a few of the elders still remember, and they pass on their memories to the tribes' younger generations. They tell of families gathering on the coast, having come by wagon and horse to gather seaweed and abalone. Salmon were caught and smoked right in camp, and tan oak acorns were smashed for soup and bread. There were dances and songs to celebrate the earth and its abundance.

A History of Loss

The elders tell of the dark times, too. During the 1850s white settlers appeared in the Sinkyone region, the red-hot fevers of gold and Manifest Destiny burning in their marrow. In an effort to "civilize" the region, the whites slaughtered thousands of Indians in a massive, genocidal campaign; bounty hunting and scalping were state- and federal-government–funded activities carried out by hired guns. In one instance a five-year-old child later known as Sally Bell hid in the bushes while U.S. soldiers massacred her mother, father, and siblings. For an interview in her later years, she recounted the atrocity: "They killed my baby sister and cut her heart out and threw it in the brush where I ran and hid. My little sister was a baby, just crawling around. I didn't know what to do. I was so scared that I guess I just hid there a long time with my little sister's heart in my hands."

But in a way Sally Bell was lucky. Many other Sinkyone children were enslaved—sold by slave traders for the "pleasures" of white society in San Francisco. Others were uprooted from their homes and forced into the humiliation of a concentration-camp environment on the Mendocino reservation. But a few escaped into the hills and were absorbed into surviving tribes.

Those survivors never forgot their history. Or their Sinkyone land.

From the periphery, the remaining Sinkyone people watched as the logging industry moved in and began to cut the ancient, sacred redwoods with which the tribes had lived in harmony for so many years. From 1950 through the mid-1980s, the great white corporate giants brought equipment that each year grew in size as well as productivity. The Sinkyone redwood rain forests disappeared as the soils ran downhill into the streams. Soon the salmon and steelhead disappeared, too. And sacred Indian cultural resources were ruthlessly churned up, flattened, and destroyed beneath the new machinery as it chewed its way through the forest.

But the 1970s ushered in a new era of hope for the Sinkyone. Although the timber industry was cutting down the northern California forests at a frantic rate, the back-to-the-land movement was transplanting to Mendocino County folks who, not unlike the local Native People, wanted their children to inherit a legacy of ancient forests. Together with the local tribal members, their outrage thundered down the coast and through the redwood forests, mobilizing a movement to save Sinkyone's last redwood trees. By the time a diorama was erected at the Sinkyone Wilderness State Park visitor center proclaiming the Sinkyone a "vanished people," the local Natives' protests were heard loud and clear. By the mid-1980s only 2 percent of the Sinkyone's old-growth redwoods remained. The environmentalists and local tribal members gathered to halt the chain-saw assault on the Sally Bell Redwood Grove—one of the last stands of old redwoods. They climbed trees and blocked bulldozers to stop the logging. They were led away in handcuffs.

Taking a Stand

Soon the two groups found themselves in the midst of a legal battle. On behalf of the local Native People, the International Indian Treaty Council, a local environmental group called the Environmental Protection Information Center (EPIC), and the Sierra Club sued the California Department of Forestry (CDF), charging that timber giant Georgia-Pacific had destroyed Sinkyone cultural sites while the CDF had failed to consider the logging operation's cumulative impacts on the watershed. The case was precedent setting: As a result, the CDF was forced to revamp its statewide guidelines for the approval of timber harvest plans.

Known as the Sally Bell Lawsuit (*EPIC v. Johnson*, July 1985), the court's decision saved 7,100 acres of Sinkyone land, including the famous Sally Bell Grove and two smaller groves, from further clear-cutting. Georgia-Pacific, realizing that its Sinkyone logging days were over, put the land up for sale. By 1986 it was purchased by the Trust for Public Land (TPL) through a loan from the California State Coastal Conservancy. Thirty-two hundred acres of coastal strip and old-growth forest were added to the adjoining Sinkyone Wilderness State Park, while the remaining 3,800 acres of second-growth redwood and Douglas fir were designated to be resold to a local public interest group—as long as the land was managed for "multiple use." The timber industry read this term to mean "industrial logging," and again clear-cutting seemed an imminent reality.

Finding Strength in Numbers

At the end of 1986, the InterTribal Sinkyone Wilderness Council was formed. This council of eleven tribes, representing some 7,000 Native Americans—many with ancestral ties to Sinkyone—issued a resounding declaration to gain back both sovereignty and stewardship of Sinkyone lands. The InterTribal Council had a vision for the land—based on a different interpretation of *multiple use*—and announced its plans for an InterTribal Sinkyone Wilderness Park. This park would restore the ancient redwood forest ecosystem while allowing for sustainable, Native American traditions to continue—a type of wilderness that included Native People in its ecosystem. The tribes saw the land as a place where their religious and cultural traditions could be handed down to their young people, whom they feared were becoming increasingly vulnerable to drugs and alcohol. The park would provide a return to traditional ways, allowing the tribes to gather their traditional foods, while protecting and restoring the historic rain forests, the coastal fisheries, the plant and animal communities, and other Native American cultural resources. It was a place where the roots of the Original People could firmly reestablish themselves among those of the great redwoods.

But the California State Coastal Conservancy wasn't certain that the InterTribal Council's definition of *multiple use* met its own or that of the communities it represented, which were full of citizens employed by the logging industry. The Council, knowing it would have to raise a great deal of money to prove that it was serious about the plan, raised $20,000 from small foundations and donations within the year.

Although it was a hopeful start, the group was going to need a whole lot more money. The property, valued at $4 million if opened to logging, would be worth considerably less if a conservation easement were put on it. But even at a discount, it was a mind-boggling amount of money—especially for a group of people who had been systematically sidelined in America's race for monetary wealth.

Reaching Out

Meanwhile, a white corporate executive was building his home just south of the Sinkyone land, near Fort Bragg—oblivious to the efforts of the tribes so near at hand. Ron Nadeau wasn't your average corporate man, though; for one thing, he was building a modest house amid a lovely transition forest of young redwoods and rhododendrons, and for another he was doing it with his own hands. He spent many weekends bent over a piece of wood, working its grain with his sander. "One morning I started to get this weird feeling," Nadeau says. Then he interrupts his own story, saying, "This is *Twilight Zone* stuff—I'm not sure if it's believable." Then he starts again. "I had this feeling that I was being watched. I would stop and look around, see nothing, and go back to work. Then it would happen again." His voice trails off as he struggles to find words for his story. "You can call it a fantasy or whatever, but there was this presence in the woods that day."

Later Nadeau was looking through the newspaper—an odd thing in itself, since he rarely read the paper. He saw an article about the Council's fight to save Sinkyone; impulsively he cut it out and tacked it up on his wall, all the while making no connection to his experience in the backyard. Nadeau felt an overwhelming urge to meet with and help the council in any way that he could. Soon he was phoning the InterTribal office, leaving messages. When Hawk Rosales, the Council's executive director, returned his call, Nadeau launched into a description of his role as a board member for Outdoor Industry Conservation Alliance (OICA). He eagerly explained how he thought he could help get funding for the land purchase.

"I have to be honest," Nadeau says. "Hawk was not real warm. When I finally asked him why he wasn't more enthusiastic about this stuff, he replied, 'We're Indians, Ron. This type of thing hardly ever pans out. It's just not where most folks put their money.'" But after repeated overtures from this unusual but compassionate white man who manufactured hand warmers for a living, Rosales agreed to meet with Nadeau and hear more.

Nadeau drove up to Ukiah, to the InterTribal Council's office. "I walked down the halls and noticed that there were these old photos of the local Indian people in traditional costume. *Here* was the connection to the presence I felt in the redwoods behind my home."

That connection made Nadeau a man obsessed. He pitched the Conservation Alliance hard to Rosales, who finally agreed to draft a proposal. "It was so weird," Nadeau says. "Usually folks are trying to sell the Alliance on their projects, but this time it was the other way around. Hawk's reticence was understandable, though. I don't think Native Americans are used to us trying to give them money to buy property."

Rosales drafted a proposal for the Alliance, which asked for $30,000 toward the purchase of the Sinkyone uplands. At the time the Council had only $20,000 in the bank for what would be at least a million-dollar acquisition.

Nadeau had never worked so hard to promote a group's efforts. By the time the OICA board met, he had personally called or met with every member, and Rosales had gotten impressive information packets into their hands. Still, the board was uncertain. Was funding a Native American land acquisition its thing? After all, the Conservation Alliance represented the outdoor recreation industry; not only did it fund projects that protected the natural world, but it tried to do so in the spirit of protecting nonmotorized recreation values as well. In most people's minds that meant climbing, mountain biking, and backpacking.

A New Direction for the Alliance

The discussion at the autumn 1993 board meeting was considerable. Some folks were opposed to the small amount of select log-

Ancient coastal forest preserved from clear-cutting by establishment of the InterTribal Sinkyone Wilderness Park.

ging that the InterTribal Council proposed in order to rehabili-
tate the forest as well as generate some cash flow. Others felt there
wasn't enough public benefit—that the opportunities for public
recreation were too limited, since most of the land would be off
limits to everyone but the local tribal members. Nadeau responded that this project was absolutely worthy of Alliance money: It
was an "underdog issue," and it was a local community concern,
both of which the group generally favored. Besides, he argued,
wasn't there an enormous spiritual component to wilderness, and
even to recreation—which Americans had come to embrace with
almost religious fervor? A thoughtful debate followed: Wasn't
recreation a sort of 're-creation'? The InterTribal wilderness
would be an example of this—a re-creation of that which had
been lost, both ecologically and culturally. Besides, buying the
land would save it from massive logging. Just because a bunch of
white guys in Lycra couldn't ride their mountain bikes through
there didn't mean that the Native People wouldn't be reaping
enormous recreational value from their time on the land.

"I have to hand it to the Conservation Alliance," Nadeau says.
"They sat at the table for hours, debating this proposal. Some
people were on board from the beginning, saying, 'It's not quite
within our guidelines, but it's about time we did something for the
Native Americans.' And others came all the way across the spectrum—from 'absolutely not' to 'maybe' and then finally to 'yes,
let's do it.' It was an extraordinary educational process for all of us,
and for the industry. A real consciousness raising. We all had to
think outside our box to see what else *recreation* might mean, to
see who else we could serve."

Within weeks of submitting the proposal, the InterTribal
Council received a check from the Conservation Alliance for
$30,000. The members couldn't believe it. The Alliance money
not only more than doubled their savings for the land but also
demonstrated a real leap of faith that brought other foundations
and donors on board. By late 1994 the Council had $100,000 in

the bank and had spent $60,000 from the Ford Foundation and private donors to produce the Sinkyone documentary film. And if this weren't enough to legitimize its cause, in December 1994 the Mendocino County Board of Supervisors voted unanimously to support the InterTribal Park plan.

Jobs Versus the Environment?

The Coastal Conservancy now had to take the Council seriously as a potential buyer. But at a March 1995 meeting, in a crowded and edgy room, timber officials leaned hard on the Conservancy with their familiar "jobs versus the environment" argument. They felt that the park proposal was a million-dollar giveaway at taxpayers' expense. It would devastate the local economy; some said they had been "stabbed in the back," because they'd been led to believe that *multiple use* meant a timber harvest. Furthermore, local families that were dependent on timber jobs would be devastated.

County Supervisor Liz Henry dismissed the loggers' arguments. The *Los Angeles Times* described her stance against the timber executives, who were famous for pressuring public agencies in order to get their way. Henry told the Coastal Conservancy "not to be swayed" by arguments that this action would crush the timber industry, adding that "there is room for diversification in Mendocino County's economy, and we feel that this one and only first intertribal park in the Sinkyone is something that will put Mendocino on the map in the world." Environmentalists at the meeting agreed, adding that the Conservancy could "make right the conscience of this country" by selling back the land to the Native People. Some even argued that it should be given back free of charge.

After six heated hours of public testimony, the Conservancy voted 5–0 in favor of transferring the land to the Council. There was one stipulation: The deal was good only if a restrictive conservation easement was in place, its language detailing exactly how many trees of a certain diameter each acre would contain, with an overriding promise to restore and maintain a mature forest. Further, this easement would state that until the forest reached such a mature state, it could be thinned at a rate of no more than 1 percent per year. This was fine with the Sinkyone Council, whose members wanted their forest to be as old and healthy as it had been in the days of their ancestors. This portion of Sinkyone would now be returned to its Original People for $1.4 million. To add to the sweet victory, the Lannan Foundation pledged up to $1.3 million to cover costs. With the $100,000 that the Conservation Alliance and others had granted, the InterTribal Sinkyone Wilderness Park had grown from seed to sprout. On August 18, 1997, the Council completed its purchase of the Sinkyone property.

It had been a decade of controversy in which many Indians and non-Indians had forged a broader definition of *multiple use* and expanded the idea of *wilderness* to include the sustainable presence and stewardship of Native People. They had also broadened the public's understanding of public and private land: Here was land that wasn't wholly private, yet didn't allow for unlimited public access. Although there would be three trails that connected with the trail systems of the adjoining Sinkyone Wilderness State Park, the remainder of the InterTribal Wilderness Park would exist only as a traditional cultural-use area for the local Native People, a place of worship and rejuvenation.

The InterTribal Sinkyone Wilderness Park was the first of its kind. Never before had so many tribes of Native Americans banded together—to establish a nonprofit organization to purchase so much land for restoration and preservation. And never before had the government transferred land to Indians under a conservation easement. "The entire indigenous world is watching," says Hawk Rosales. "If we can establish this model of Native control and stewardship of returned land, it will have a great impact on other Native Peoples around the globe who have been overwhelmed and dispossessed."

Justice and Healing

The Trust for Public Land, which had been holding the land for the Coastal Conservancy, was elated with the happy ending. TPL president Will Rogers says, "The transfer of these lands to Indian people is an act of social and environmental justice." Ron Nadeau, who had attended community meetings and cheered from the sidelines throughout the process, can't agree more. "There have been so many massacres on, and to, that land. It's the very least we could do to help make things right again."

In *The Run to Save Sinkyone*, the camera trains its eye on several Council spokespeople. Each speaks in an effort to help the viewer understand their collective vision for their ancestral land and its redwood rain forests. "We need to rely on the basis of Native wisdom, which was developed over thousands of years' time," one says. "And that came from a close relationship . . . with the land, every day. And understanding you're not above it. You're part of it."

It is true. We are all part of it—even those of us who will never set foot in the forests of Sinkyone. We can still be witness to a long-overdue healing, a restoration of roots to soil.

BIBLIOGRAPHY

InterTribal Sinkyone Wilderness Council. *InterTribal Sinkyone Wilderness Council Land Acquisition Proposal.* Ukiah, Calif.: InterTribal Sinkyone Wilderness Council, 1993.

———. *The Run to Save Sinkyone.* Produced, written, and directed by Jonathan L. Rosales. 46 min. Desert Waters Productions, in association with Kifaru Productions, 1994. Videocassette.

———. "The Vision and the Work." *California Coast & Ocean,* autumn 1996, 12–14.

"Native Americans to Acquire Land for a Coast Redwood Park," *Los Angeles Times,* 12 April 1995.

Nomland, Gladys Ayer. *Sinkyone Notes.* Berkeley, Calif.: University of California Press, 1935.

Poole, William. "Return of the Sinkyone." *Land and People,* spring 1998, 18–20.

———. "Return of the Sinkyone." *Sierra,* November/December 1996.

"Tribes Join for Tribute to Indian Life," *San Francisco Chronicle,* 23 May 1995.

"In a Northern California Forest, Indians Take Back the Land," *Washington Post,* 7 October 1997.

Full Circle

The South Yuba River, California
1983–1999

Born as an iridescent sliver of water in California's High Sierras, the South Yuba is fattened with the help of the nation's heaviest snowfalls. Farther downstream enormous white boulders and gorges are stark against the verdant water of the river—you can see through the green glass to the bottom of twenty-foot-deep pools. Slates, schists, marbles, and quartzites line the canyon floor, once a softer stone at the bottom of a Paleozoic sea.

In *Turtle Island*, Pulitzer Prize–winning poet Gary Snyder paid tribute to this stretch of free-flowing water and its rich physical and cultural histories—including a wave of harsh human abuses. His book was portentous: Just a few years later, local citizens would discover that the river was again under siege as developers produced countless new proposals to dam its waters. It was unthinkable that this river and its corridor—which served as the spiritual epicenter of the Nevada County community, offered Class III, IV, and V rafting and kayaking, and defined a 39-mile spur of the Pacific Rim Trail—could all be entombed behind a massive concrete wall. And those were just the tangible human losses—it was impossible to quantify the number of species and habitats that might vanish forever.

A Poetic History

"What Happened Here Before" describes an extraordinary watershed and how it arrived at its present-day condition. Snyder's words wander through history, falling like water and carving out

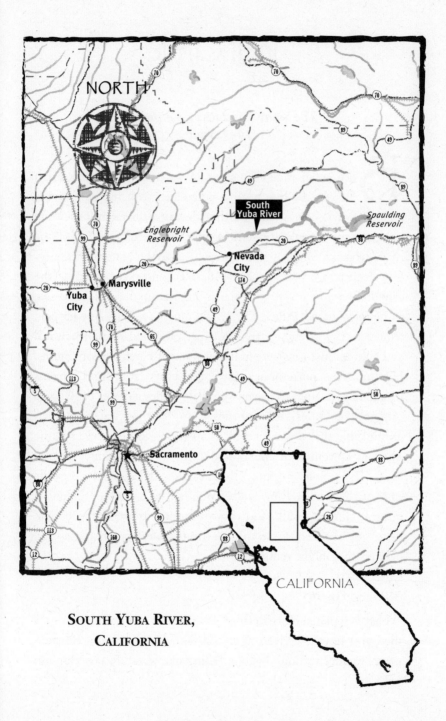

NORTH

70

70

70

49

89

South
Yuba River

Spaulding
Reservoir

49

89

80

Englebright
Reservoir

Nevada
City

89

70

99

20

174

26

Marysville

49

Yuba
City

26

49

70

99

65

80

113

49

56

5

99

56

Sacramento

88

80

5

26

113

99

160

88

12

12

CALIFORNIA

**SOUTH YUBA RIVER,
CALIFORNIA**

meaning the way the South Yuba has carved out the thick granite canyons of northern California.

The poet describes his homeland on the South Yuba River as it was 40,000 years ago, when the first people, the Nisenan, lived sparingly off the land. Their community and culture celebrated the earth rather than dominated it; wildlife and fish were thick beyond our modern imagination:

> . . . *And human people came with basket hats and nets*
> *winter-houses underground*
> *yew bows painted green,*
> *feasts and dances for the boys and girls*
> *songs and stories in the smoky dark . . .*

Then, after eons of ecological harmony, in just 125 years, the white man's frenzy for gold resulted in atrocities. With the advent of hydraulic mining, entire mountains were washed down the river and into the Central Valley—the silt deposited along the way raised the lower South Yuba's riverbed by 110 feet. Excessive logging of the old-growth forests undressed the hillsides and left them lifeless, while the new white settlements drove off or killed the Native People.

Finally Snyder turns to the present, writing of a new enlightened era in which the South Yuba has begun to recover and many humans embrace the river as something sacred—in a Buddhist sort of way—that exists on its own terms outside of any human need:

> . . . *the land belongs to itself.*
> *"no self in self; no self in things" . . .*

It was indeed this new cultural understanding of nature that saved the river. In 1983 a local man named Dennis Barry saw in the newspapers that the South Yuba was threatened by dam proposals. In a process known as "water ranching," developers were interested in harvesting the river's water to sell to the highest bidder, usually hot, dry southwestern suburbs with lots of lawns to water.

Barry immediately sat down and wrote a letter to the editor, objecting to any further industrial development on the Yuba, one of California's best and last free-flowing streams between Spaulding and Englebright dams. That same night another local, Linda Miller, was stewing over the news as well. "Instead of the familiar 'somebody ought to do something about that,' I found myself saying 'Oh no they're not,'" she recalls. "I had no idea what to do about it but they were *not* going to [dam the river]!"

The Circle Forms

With one phone call from Miller to Barry, the South Yuba River Citizens' League began to form. Miller prefers the acronym, SYRCL; it inspires the image of people banding together on behalf of their community. According to Barry, the circle of citizens just snowballed. "There were a lot more people like us than we realized . . . there were people that said, 'This is one of the most beautiful spots we've ever seen and we're not going to let it get destroyed.'"

Dr. Roger Hicks, a local doctor, was appointed the volunteer leader of SYRCL, and in the group's first decade it successfully fought off five dam proposals. By 1989 the organization had attracted several hundred members and was able to hire an actual staff person—Kerri Varian became SYRCL's first executive director.

SYRCL's members were relentless, but their defensive approach—fighting individual dam proposals—was like chasing their own tail. It was also time consuming and draining. In 1986 SYRCL's citizens decided it was time to get proactive and stop for good the endless cycle of proposed future dams. They launched a campaign to seek state-based Wild and Scenic River designation, which would automatically protect against the small dams or diversion projects they had been fighting. The state program was a spin-off of the federal Wild and Scenic Rivers Act passed in 1968 to balance dam development with long-term protection of exceptional free-flowing rivers across the United States.

SYRCL's citizens succeeded in getting a bill introduced before the California State Assembly, but development interests washed the legislation away. Refusing to be defeated, SYRCL dug in its heels and looked for other ways to protect the river. After volunteers gathered 9,000 signatures, Proposition 70 was hatched, and eventually it was passed in 1988. The result: $2,000,000 was appropriated to acquire lands from willing sellers along the South Yuba—to be managed as South Yuba State Park. SYRCL then assisted the California State Parks Department by using its own donated funds to lease lands up for sale until the department could round up the money appropriated under Prop 70 and buy the land outright. But just as it began to look as if SYRCL was making headway, the Yuba County Water Agency announced plans to sell off $8,000,000 worth of Yuba water. Its preliminary proposal, released in 1989, highlighted plans for four new dams—which would bury more than half of the free stretch of the South Yuba at taxpayers' expense.

Going Federal

At this point SYRCL was skilled at grassroots organizing efforts: making educational presentations and presenting testimony at scheduled hearings. Members kept the work going at a full boil, and cooked up a new legislative campaign as well. This time the group sought federal Wild and Scenic status; only the federal level of protection could stop a project of this magnitude. SYRCL's first step was to ask why the Tahoe National Forest had failed to consider studying a single river for Wild and Scenic status in its Land and Resource Management Plan. To the group's delight, the agency admitted that it hadn't followed its own guidelines. Under public pressure, the Forest Service promised to revisit the study and revise its recommendations accordingly. Still, SYRCL feared that the agency's study would be tainted by pressure from development interests. So through small foundation grants and donations, SYRCL members initiated their own suitability study for

A stretch of the South Yuba proposed for hydropower development.

the South Yuba, which resulted in a 180-page document. They also began aggressively recruiting endorsements from local private property owners, business owners, and residents to demonstrate the community's support for Wild and Scenic River status. Soon the group had assembled an impressive cast of characters made up not only of back-to-the-land hippie types but also of mainstreamers, including 155 business owners, 83 realtors, 30 lawyers, dozens of teachers, and 109 landowners with property bordering the river. In April 1993 SYRCL presented a petition with these endorsers' signatures to the Nevada County Board of Supervisors, asking that the county voice its support for Wild and Scenic designation. The county, under pressure from development interests, stalled—deferring its decision until the Forest Service had completed its suitability study.

Drowning in "Wise-Use" Rhetoric

Indeed, pressure from SYRCL's opponents was mounting. Fresh from a Montana "Wise Use" conference, a local developer rallied property owners to form the California Landowners Alliance. Their handbook, *The Fight to Beat a Wild and Scenic River Designation*, had been put out by the New Hampshire Landowners Alliance. An offshoot of the Alliance for America—a national anti-environmental group funded by the American Farm Bureau Federation, American Mining Congress, American Petroleum Institute, and other development proponents—the New Hampshire group, which had deep pockets, had successfully killed several proposals for Wild and Scenic River designations in the East using grassroots tactics borrowed from environmental and other socially progressive groups.

SYRCL was shocked. The group had worked within the mainstream community for nearly ten years, and overnight it had been marginalized. According to Kerri Varian, SYRCL staff, supporters, and volunteers were accused of being "fanatics, ecofreaks, and radical environmentalists engaged in collusions and racketeering to gain personal control over the South Yuba." An anti-SYRCL canvassing effort was launched; canvassers went door to door telling residents of the river corridor that if the river was designated Wild and Scenic, the federal government would take away their land or limit their use of it—even though a federal study had just concluded that no private property had ever been condemned along a federal Wild and Scenic River in California.

Then the phone calls began. An anonymous caller contacted the business owners who had endorsed SYRCL and threatened a boycott if they continued to support the group and its agenda for river protection. Harassing calls were made to SYRCL staff, both at work and at home. Another individual associated with the Landowners Alliance threatened to sue SYRCL if it didn't supply him with its mailing list.

Now the group not only had to continue its proactive Wild and Scenic campaign, but it also needed to countercampaign against the Wise-Use rhetoric, which was confusing many friends of the river. Kerri Varian was running the organization on a $75,000 annual budget derived mostly from the contributions of folks who lived in California's poorest and most unemployed county. With trepidation, Varian went back to the community, in the hope of finding a deep pocket she had somehow missed.

She found it in the unlikely form of a tiny local business. AlpineAire Quality Foods, a maker of backpacking meals, had done its best to support SYRCL from the beginning and continued to publicly endorse the group despite pressure from members of the California Landowners Alliance. Committed to protection of the natural world, AlpineAire had also recently joined the Outdoor Industry Conservation Alliance (OICA) and now had an opportunity to help SYRCL obtain the level of support it needed.

Varian sent a proposal to the Alliance, stapled to AlpineAire's letter of support. In it she explained SYRCL's situation vis-à-vis the Wise Users and outlined her plan for dealing with anti-environmental rhetoric. "Wise Use has picked the wrong arena for its lies and deceits," she wrote in the proposal's introduction. "Not only do we plan to beat Wise Use here on the South Yuba, we will document our efforts and their outcomes for use as a case study by conservation organizations and natural resource protection efforts around the country."

The Conservation Alliance liked that kind of spirit and recognized the vital role the South Yuba played in northern California's ecosystems and human communities. Ron Nadeau, who was president of the Conservation Alliance at the time, wrote a letter to SYRCL filled with encouragement for the difficult work it was doing. Enclosed was a check for $30,000—almost half of what SYRCL had hoped to spend that year.

Gaining Steam

SYRCL and its supporters were ecstatic. Such a grant meant more time winning protection for the river and less time scraping together funding. The group launched headfirst into community action, organizing raft trips, watershed hikes, and river cleanups. It created a Private Property Owners' Committee comprised of forty landowners, and began an Adopt-a-Watershed program for teachers and students. Soon SYRCL was as deep in the soul of the community as the river was—the energy and character of the water and the people inextricably intertwined.

With resources from the OICA in hand, SYRCL was able to recruit even more business owners, buoying its argument for Wild and Scenic River designation. By this time SYRCL had even gained enough stature to be given a "community" seat at the Economic Enhancement Roundtable, a civic group made up of the regions' movers and shakers, and was welcomed into the Nevada City Chamber of Commerce.

Dr. Roger Hicks was still a crucial part of SYRCL's board and proud of what the group had accomplished as well as the dignified, yet flexible style it had adapted—which allowed for quick changes of strategy at difficult junctures. "SYRCL faced tremendous adversity during this period from opponents trying to undermine the group's good standing in the community," he says. "But in the face of it all, SYRCL maintained the high road, doing everything possible to bring people together instead of pulling them apart." In his mind, "SYRCL's acceptance into the local business community through the EER and the Nevada City Chamber of Commerce just proved that the approach was working."

Gary Snyder's influence continued long after his poem about his home was published. As a member of SYRCL's advisory board, he brought a kind of Zen compassion and calm to both conservation and community issues that helped set the tenor of the organization during a difficult time. As a result, despite the heated frenzy around them, the folks at SYRCL kept their cool and their grace under fire.

Other events helped float the group's sense of accomplishment. In August 1996 the Forest Service released the anxiously awaited revised suitability study for the South Yuba and other rivers it had overlooked the first time around. This time, with the citizens' study as reinforcement, the agency recommended designating all 39 free-flowing miles of the South Yuba as Wild and Scenic. It was a terrific intermediate victory for SYRCL—and validation of everything the group had been saying for thirteen years running.

New Obstacles

But the opposition had gotten to the county supervisors, who voted 4–1 not to support designation of *any* river in the Tahoe National Forest. SYRCL knew that local support wasn't necessary for the designation—but it would definitely help. And it had to get the river protected before any more dam proposals were seriously considered. Along with its own twelve-page comment, SYRCL's citizens penned more than 1,000 letters demonstrating their support for the Forest Service's draft recommendation.

Then Mother Nature kicked in with some ill-timed antics. On

New Year's weekend, 1997, northern California suffered from a series of devastating floods; 100,000 people were evacuated from their homes, many of which were destroyed. In what was already an impoverished region, the folks downstream screamed for better flood protection. The people who sold water for a living drew attention to the tragedy and called for two new dams at an expense totaling over $1.3 billion to be built on the lower Yuba. SYRCL responded that the dams would flood one of the Central Valley's last remaining salmon and steelhead runs—a popular fishing location. They would also drown a wildlife preserve, a nationally renowned hunting ground, and a University of California research station. Linking arms with Cal-Trout and the Bureau of Land Management (BLM), SYRCL produced an alternative flood-control plan—one that would cost considerably less while providing opportunities to enhance the local economy. The proposal described a 20-mile parkway along the river, from Marysville to the Englebright dam, and achieved flood control through an improved levee and slurry wall system. The plan was augmented by a recent U.S. Army Corps of Engineers study, which had concluded that dams on the Yuba River were economically, technically, and environmentally unfeasible.

Despite SYRCL's concurrent efforts to help flood victims, members found themselves accused of being unresponsive to the needs of the people—for loving a river more than their fellow humans. Meanwhile, the Yuba County Water Agency initiated a $700,000 campaign to lay the groundwork for a slew of dams and diversions on the Yuba. The race between more dams and Wild and Scenic designation was on. Members of the Conservation Alliance watched from the sidelines, holding their breath. It was an anxious time: The Alliance had watched SYRCL come so far, and it hated to see the plug pulled on the group for lack of funds. At the end of 1997, Ron Nadeau himself, along with his hand-warmer company, Grabber Performance Group, sponsored another proposal from SYRCL. The Alliance rushed to give the group another check, this time for $35,000.

Enter Shawn Garvey, a long-time campaign organizer for California's Senate races. After a year's sabbatical during which he founded an independent film festival in Vermont, he found himself longing for the West Coast again. One night, sifting through job announcements on the Internet, he found that SYRCL desperately needed a new executive director. Soon Garvey found himself back in California, picking up where Kerri Varian left off. He was ready to spend some serious time at the California State Legislature, in the hope that passage of a state-level Wild and Scenic bill would spur federal protection, too. SYRCL was in luck: While the organization was restricted from using most other foundation funds to lobby decision makers, the Conservation Alliance made it clear that its money could be used in full for such an effort.

Storming California's State Capitol

The new resources and expertise came just in time because the Northern California Water Association had hired the state's most highly paid lobbyist to fight protective designation for the South Yuba River. SYRCL's new campaign director, John Regan, acting with the calm, fluid cachet of the organization, shrugged off the threat that the lobbyist posed, saying to the local newspapers, "It feels a bit like David vs. Goliath, but we all know who won that fight." Then SYRCL's opponents arrived at the State Capitol in Sacramento, arguing that dams would save them from future floods. Their mascot was Rodeo, a dog made famous during the 1997 floods, when an entire nation had glued itself to the television watching Rodeo's helicopter rescue from the roof of a submerged home. It was a stunt designed to tug at the heartstrings of politicians and press alike. One of SYRCL's most dedicated activists, Izzy Martin, responded: "I can't help but notice that some of the people opposing our bill . . . are also opposing flood-control money being put into the water bond."

The floodgates had opened. Supported by a third Conservation

Shawn Garvey (top left) and fellow SYRCL members celebrate Governor Gray Davis's signing of the Wild and Scenic Bill on October 10, 1999.

Alliance grant, SYRCL kept the pressure on during the Wild and Scenic bill's eleventh hour in the capitol. And State Senator Byron Sher (a Democrat from Stanford) remained unfazed by the flack he was getting for championing the bill to protect the South Yuba. "These free-flowing rivers are much like the coast of California," Senator Sher said to the *Union* newspaper. "These are assets . . . to all the people of California." Indeed, *assets* seemed to be the word du jour: Working Assets, a long-distance telephone company, announced that it would provide its customers with free long-distance phone time to call Mary Nichols, the secretary of the California Resources Agency, in support of Wild and Scenic designation for the river. Working Assets' citizens' action director, Janet Nudelman, told the *Union* that the company had not been asked to support the bill; it chose the issue independently after researching the proposed dam projects and determining that the idea was "as crazy as it looked."

Sure enough, Senator Sher's bill for Wild and Scenic designation passed in the Senate and the House—it had only to be signed by the governor. The *San Francisco Chronicle* editorialized that "Sen. Sher says SB496 is one of the most important environmental bills to be considered . . . this year, and he could be right. It is supported by an array of environmental and sporting groups, including the Wilderness Society, the Sierra Club, the National Resources Defense Council, the Audubon Society, and two-thirds of the private property owners in the river canyon." The newspaper denounced the bill's opponents who argued that they needed flood control by referring to the Army Corps of Engineers' determination that 300-year flood protection could be achieved merely by improving existing levees. The editorial ended with a plea to Governor Gray Davis to sign the bill—which he did, just nine days later.

A Recipe for Victory

How did they win? Shawn Garvey grins, saying only three words: "Music and beer." Then he adds, "It was all about building community around a sense of place. Here, the South Yuba River is that place." Garvey confesses that he, like most of the SYRCL staff, is so busy working to stop dams and other projects, that he only actually gets to the river's edge about eight times a year. "But when I look at the name of our organization, the part of South

Yuba River Citizens' League that rings true for me is the idea of 'citizen.' For years I have searched for a community in which to belong, and from the very first day, I could feel that Nevada City was home. The river has given so much soul to this community, and it reached out and just drew me in."

By 2000 SYRCL's ranks had expanded to 3,650 members—the largest membership in the nation for an organization working to protect a single river. And it was this union of friends and neighbors and businesses, forged by time, effort, and resolve, that had formed the most formidable barrier for developers seeking to use the river for their own ends. Dennis Barry said that "people who are fighting to save the South Yuba feel like if they can hang on to [this river], they can hang on to the world." It was testament to the strength of the circle.

Shawn Garvey takes his hat off to the members of the Conservation Alliance. "They were with us for the long run. They had faith in our plan in the beginning, and then sustained us in the critical years afterward. If they had pulled the plug after the first year, we never would have had the financial endurance to see this thing through."

The citizens' campaign to save the South Yuba River leads us to ask bigger, bolder questions such as *How many more rivers can we sacrifice?* Or, better yet, *How many can we save?* Gary Snyder's "What Happened Here Before" prompts related questions: *What kind of culture do we want to be? At what expense?*

BIBLIOGRAPHY

Finnegan, Lora J. "Ramble Along the River." *Sunset,* September 1999: 43–44.

McClurg, Sue. "The South Yuba: One River, Two Visions." *Western Water,* July/August 1999: 4–13.

Schiffner, Gregg. *Stories of the Yuba: A Filmmaker's Journey on the River of his Youth.* Produced and directed by Gregg Schiffner. 75 min. Gandl Productions, 1998.

Snyder, Gary. *A Place in Space: Ethics, Aesthetics, and Watersheds.* Washington, D.C.: Counterpoint, 1995.

———. *Turtle Island.* 1969. Reprint, New York: New Directions Books, 1974.

"South Fork of Yuba River Should Be 'Wild and Scenic,'" *San Francisco Chronicle,* 1 October 1999.

South Yuba River Citizens' League. "Conservation Alliance Proposals." Nevada City, Calif.: South Yuba Citizens' League, 1994, 1997, 1999.

———. *The South Yuba: A Wild and Scenic River Report.* Nevada City, Calif.: South Yuba River Citizens' League, 1993.

———. SYRCL *Watershed Protection and Restoration Since 1983.* Nevada City, Calif.: South Yuba River Citizens' League, 1998.

———. "Wild and Scenic Is the Law!" *Views* 18, No. 1 (Jan. 2000).

Union (Grass Valley and Nevada City, Calif.), 19 February–2 September 1999.

Viva la Tortuga!

Sea Turtles on the South Texas Coast
1982–2000

Rancho Nuevo, Mexico, 1947

Las madres came in droves, an ancient, internal compass guiding them through the Gulf's waters and onto the bone-colored sands of the remote Rancho Nuevo. By the thousands their hundred-pound gray-green bodies emerged from the waves. It was an arduous trek across the dunes; their grace in the water turned to grudge work on the land.

A silent meditation shimmered in the air as the females advanced across the beach. Heckling gulls jabbed at their heads; coyotes and vultures circled around and above. The sun's heat fell hard on their shells. The local *hombres* kicked at them, rode astride their broad backs. But the ancient matriarchs kept their steady pace without a blink or falter. They were going to give their young a chance, even if it cost them their lives.

A Mexican rancher was there that day. With an 8-millimeter camera, he filmed the mile-long *arribada de las tortugas* (arrival of the turtles). He filmed the spherical promises of life that tumbled from their bellies, and the locals who kneeled behind the nesting turtles to snatch their eggs as they dropped. Little did Señor Herrera know that he had just recorded history, a history that was dying as quickly as the mothers could dig their nests.

On that single afternoon 40,000 sea turtles nested at Rancho Nuevo. By 1977 just thirty years later, only 250 turtles a day returned to the last nesting place in the world for the Kemp's ridley sea turtle.

NORTH

Houston

Gulf of
Mexico

Port Aransas
Corpus Christi

Kingsville

Padre Island
National
Seashore

Port Mansfield

South
Padre Island
Port Isabel
Brownsville
Matamoros

Rio Grande

TEXAS

MEXICO

PADRE ISLAND
NATIONAL SEASHORE,
TEXAS

TEXAS

Houston, Texas, 1982

Carole Allen was a full-time mother who wanted her daughter to see the natural world and all its creatures; to understand the intricate quilt of life. In Texas such lessons were difficult to teach: The livestock on the ranches at the fringes of Houston was about the closest thing to wildlife anyone ever saw anymore. But Allen was a persistent woman. She persuaded her daughter's grade school principal to arrange a Saturday field trip to the Galveston Laboratory of the National Marine Fisheries Service (NMFS), 70 miles away. She wanted her daughter and the other children to see the sea turtles, *las tortugas del mar*.

Two hundred schoolkids and parents arrived in a caravan of cars. There, near the shores of the Gulf of Mexico, they witnessed Operation Head Start, a partnership project between Mexico and several U.S. agencies designed to replenish the dwindling numbers of Kemp's ridley turtles. The scene was straight from prehistory. Staff and volunteers hovered over hundreds of tiny black reptiles, some paddling frantically in the water, others floating motionless. From the buckets that held them captive, they looked up at their caretakers, not knowing they were history in the making.

Carole Allen knelt down next to her daughter to get a closer look at the newly hatched sea turtles. Some of the parents on the field trip wrinkled their noses at the small creatures, but Allen saw them differently. There were so many, each hardly larger than a sand dollar. Even in this nascent stage, Allen could see in each pair of eyes a sentient being with a soul as old as the earth.

The Mystery of the Kemp's Ridley

Only seven kinds of sea turtles remain in the world's oceans. All are considered endangered. At an average of one hundred pounds and only two feet long, the Kemp's ridley (*Lepidochelys kempi*) is the smallest and most imperiled species. The small *tortuga* has lived behind a veil of mystery: For most of the last century, no one knew where it nested, and its migratory pattern was undecipherable. All that was really known about the turtles' movement was that they returned to their birthplace to nest, and that this course was etched deep in their memories, unalterable. Named for the man who sent a specimen to a Harvard scientist in 1880, for a long time the Kemp's ridley was considered the "bastard turtle," a hybrid of the loggerhead and the green turtle. Fishermen knew it only as the "heartbreak turtle," because more than any other species, the Kemp's ridley would struggle violently when captured and then die a dramatic death, as if from a broken heart.

An endangered Kemp's ridley nesting.

Thanks to Señor Herrera's film of the massive nesting site near Rancho Nuevo, two *gringos* finally solved the ridley riddle. One, University of Florida biologist Archie Carr, paid tribute to the film's significance in his book *The Sea Turtle: So Excellent a Fishe.* He wrote that the film proved these *tortugas* were in fact their own distinct species—characterized by their massive nesting efforts, which occurred in broad daylight. Other turtles nested alone and under the cloak of night.

It used to be that most turtle attrition occurred among eggs and hatchlings. Many of the sand-covered eggs were gobbled from their holes by coyote and other scavengers—and those that did hatch were often preyed upon by ghost crabs and birds as they headed to the water for their baptismal swim. Egg thieves, or *hueveros*, also gathered the eggs, which were sold to be savored in soups and as aphrodisiacs. The remaining babies that survived the trek across the sand usually became fish food within the first year. Optimistically, only one of the original hundred eggs laid by each female survived to adulthood.

By 1977 the Kemp's ridley was about to go the way of the dinosaurs. Despite aggressive international conservation efforts, the population continued to drop annually by 3 percent—making it one of the twelve most endangered animals in the world. And with only one official nesting colony remaining, the species would be doomed if a hurricane or an oil spill demolished that Mexican beach. So beginning in 1978 with a gift of 2,000 Kemp's ridley eggs from the Mexican government, Operation Head Start attempted to reestablish a second nesting colony at Padre Island National Seashore off the coast of Texas—the Kemp's ridleys and other sea turtles had nested there before the expansion of the U.S. shrimp industry. The ridley eggs were airlifted from Rancho Nuevo to the U.S. side of the Gulf so that they could incubate in Padre Island sand. Next, the hatchlings were taken to the NMFS lab in Galveston, where they were raised for about ten months before they were released. At that point the research team hoped the little turtles would imprint the Texas beach onto their navigational systems and return there to lay their own eggs.

In *The Great Ridley Rescue*, Pamela Phillips recounts the early days of the Head Start program. Amid barely functioning planes, monsoon storms, and emergency beach landings, she tells of a group of individuals who nearly killed themselves to deliver the temperature-controlled eggs to Padre Island National Seashore, where the eggs were hatched. In one instance, the eggs were delivered safely despite one airplane catching on fire and a second flight in which the pilot had to use a flashlight to read the instrument panels. The batch he delivered had a remarkable 91.6 percent hatch rate.

Helping Kids Help Turtles

Until their field trip to the Head Start facilities, Carole Allen and the others didn't have a clue how serious the problem was. "We just sat and watched the baby turtles swimming in the buckets, feeling helpless," Allen says. "The kids kept asking the park staff what they could do to help."

Allen was as eager to assist as the kids were. She felt the turtles had been around far longer than humans, and they certainly deserved to keep on living. As a child she, too, had been intrigued by turtles, and as an adult she felt that they served as powerful beacons to guide her. Various turtle figures decorated her home. One of her favorites is made of leather, the beadwork on its back hand-stitched by a Native American woman as a tribute to the longevity of the turtle in American Indian lore. She was also familiar with the Asian symbol of a heron standing on the back of a turtle. This illustrates the belief that all life is shouldered and sustained by Turtle Island—a single, irreplaceable island. These were symbols a mother could relate to.

Never one to passively let the world go by, Allen suggested to the kids that they could really do some good for the infant turtles by raising money to keep them fed over time. Every child, including her daughter, went for the idea. Allen gives the kids the credit for naming their group: HEART, or Help Endangered Animals— Ridley Turtles. They had been inspired by the hatchlings' heart-shaped shells.

The kids themselves had a lot of heart. With Allen's help they raised enough money to buy a special turtle chow formulated and produced by Purina, and they wrote to legislators to ask for help in saving the last of the gentle sea creatures. A Texas reporter caught wind of their efforts and wrote the story up in a Houston newspaper. HEART's fame spread across the country, *arribada* style. Soon hundreds of classrooms were contacting Allen, each wanting to form its own HEART chapter. She involved some in fund-raising efforts; if the children were from a less affluent community, she would engage them in letter writing to decision makers. Afterward Allen sent the kids a HEART certificate to display on the wall of their classroom.

Donations from businesses and individuals started rolling in as well. Allen set up a nonprofit organization to handle the funds and keep things on the straight and narrow for the IRS. But she never took a penny for herself; in the eighteen years that Allen has spent running HEART, she has always done so as a volunteer. Soon Allen and others were on the road presenting the Kemp's ridley story to thousands of classrooms, clubs, and scout groups. "I loved those days, working solely with the kids. Education of children is the main thing. They need to know what their world is about, how fragile the environment is, and how their actions impact it," she says.

A New Enemy Arrives

They were promising times, and it seemed that the ridleys' survival was assured by several factors: Operation Head Start's hatching, imprinting, and release of older and stronger turtles; the establishment of a sea turtle preserve and no-fishing zone at the Rancho Nuevo nesting beach; and the inclusion of all sea turtles on the 1973 Endangered Species List. But by the mid-1980s the entire global population of Kemp's ridley females totaled less than 500; the days of the *arribadas* were gone. Now just a few *madres* at a time would straggle onto the beach to nest. And by this point it wasn't just the eggs and hatchlings that were experiencing attrition: A record number of adult turtles had been caught in shrimp trawling nets, and others had fallen victim to hard-to-detect ghost nets and boat propellers. Many of the ridleys that were washing up dead on the shore were gravid females that were on their way to the Texas shores to nest.

Then the unimaginable happened: The U.S. government axed the Head Start program. Had legislators cut its funding because none of the program's turtles had yet returned to Padre Island to nest? HEART members responded that given the program's short life span and the time it takes for the turtles to reach reproductive maturity, the Texas-hatched turtles would need a few more years before they'd be old enough to return to nest. The National Marine Fisheries Service and the U.S. Fish and Wildlife Service would not change their decision; Operation Head Start was over before it could see the fruits of its labor.

A One-Woman Show

Allen had experienced other heartbreaks of her own. Her husband had recently died, and she had returned to the workforce to make sure her daughter could go to college. Despite her hectic schedule, though, she became convinced that teaching children about the heartbreak turtle wasn't enough anymore. There was so much more to do—and no way would she give up on the little ridleys, no matter how her personal life had evolved. "That's when the hard work started," Allen remembers. "We knew we had to go after the major cause of sea turtle mortality. A recent study by the National Research Council had established that catching and drowning in shrimp trawls was the number one cause of death among Kemp's ridleys and other sea turtles. We knew this because every year when shrimp trawling was closed, the number of sea turtles found dead on U.S. beaches went down. And as soon as shrimping season began again, the number of fatalities would go right back up."

HEART turned reluctantly from kids to Congress. Along with other marine conservation groups it had befriended, HEART began lobbying for legislation that required all U.S. shrimpers to use turtle excluder devices (TEDs) on their vessels. Installing a TED on a trawl net allowed sea turtles and other marine life to escape. Used properly, TEDs were 97 percent effective at releasing the air-breathing turtles alive. Without a TED on a trawl net, however, an enmeshed sea turtle would be unable to surface. As a result, it suffocated rather than drowned—a sphincter muscle in its air passage would remain involuntarily closed as long as it was submerged in water.

After a difficult campaign Congress passed the TED law—effective May 1, 1989. Shrimpers were outraged, arguing that the law would mean a loss of jobs and reduction of the shrimp catch. "You could have taken those stories in the papers about the little spotted owl and the loggers in the Northwest and replaced the words *owl* and *logger* with *sea turtles* and *shrimp fishermen*—and it would have been the exact same story," Allen observes. "But it was ridiculous. The shrimp populations were dwindling from overfishing and the rising cost of fuel, and the industry was faced with importing of shrimp and other problems they wanted to blame on the turtles."

Recreational anglers were complaining about the lack of fish, too. Allen points to shrimpers as the guilty party in that scenario as well. "The dead turtles were considered part of the by-catch that was brought up with the shrimp, but all sorts of other marine life, including sport and food fish, were caught in the trawlers, too." She adds, "Shrimping is a very wasteful industry, which—on its very best behavior—brings up four pounds of by-catch for every one pound of marketable shrimp. The by-catch, most of which is dead, is just thrown overboard."

By 1990 Allen had earned quite a reputation in Texas, and she was still coming at the Kemp's ridley issue aggressively. But the rest of the marine conservation community had moved on to new projects, thinking that the TEDs had saved the Kemp's in the Gulf. Allen knew better, and she was frustrated that the effort was losing steam.

That same year Allen was invited to the Mexican Presidential Palace, where the Mexican government was announcing an order that made it illegal to kill sea turtles in Mexico's waters. It was a festive occasion, and a fortuitous one for Allen. It was there that she met Todd Steiner, the director of Sea Turtle Restoration Project (STRP), an international conservation program based in San Francisco. She remembered how impressed she had been with him and STRP's projects a few years later in 1994, when sea turtle deaths along the Texas coast began to skyrocket—many of which were Kemp's ridleys. It was then that she called Steiner and reintroduced herself, explaining just how much trouble the Texas turtles were in, while no one was doing a thing about it. The national environmental groups had turned away, the state was apathetic, and the turtles were still dying. Even the National Marine Fisheries Service was hesitant to blame the shrimp industry; it told Allen that the deaths had been caused by the same virus that was causing a dolphin die-off, despite much evidence to the contrary. She asked if there was anything STRP could do.

Steiner explained that he wasn't sure if STRP was the best group to help her—it did mostly international and national work, and such a localized project was a bit off base. But he promised to look into the issue and get back to her.

New Allies

It didn't take much research before the STRP staff realized that Allen had a real crisis on her hands. A partnership was born. Before the year was out, the two groups had filed a lawsuit asking the NMFS to halt all shrimping in the Gulf of Mexico until the agency could act on behalf of the turtles and begin enforcing the use of TEDs on ships. A whole series of similar legal motions were filed the following year. Still, the NMFS insisted that the Coast Guard was getting nearly perfect TED compliance on shrimp trawlers; therefore, there must be some other reason that the turtles kept dying.

With Carole Allen's eyes and ears on the front line gathering information, STRP didn't buy it. In 1997 HEART and STRP were joined by the Humane Society of the United States, which organized an undercover investigation that eventually determined that nearly half the shrimp vessels inspected in Texas waters had purposefully disabled their turtle excluder devices. Some shrimpers had even sewn shut the escape doors.

Things looked bleak. As the year drew to a close, nine dead turtles washed up on shore—and six of them were Kemp's ridleys. Most had had their heads and flippers slashed off with straight-edge cuts—mutilations made by a knife. At least one had a chain attached to it, in an effort to send it to an ocean-floor grave. Infuriated, HEART, STRP, and the Humane Society posted a $5,000 reward for "information leading to the arrest and conviction of shrimpers caught mutilating sea turtles." In a letter to the National Marine Fisheries Service, they also demanded a shrimping ban. The shrimping industry continued to declare its innocence, and the NMFS defended its enforcement efforts, pointing to its TED patrols and an investigation into the chain-weighted turtle.

Yet other turtle news was more encouraging. In the past thirteen years, the Kemp's ridley nesting population in Mexico appeared to have increased by almost 50 percent—from 2,000 adults in 1985 to nearly 3,000 by the late 1990s. And the staff and volunteers at Padre Island National Seashore were doing great educational work with the public as well as continuously patrolling the beaches where the hatchlings had been imprinted for ten years. Among the dedicated volunteers were Mina Williams and Venice Scheurich, two retired community college teachers who helped with both turtle research and protection. Scheurich, a math and statistics teacher for thirty years, entered the satellite tracking data and recorded the weight of the hatchlings as they emerged from their shells. During nesting season she took on the most serious job of all—patrolling the beach in search of nesters. Once a mother was found, volunteers protected her while she laid her eggs; and once she returned to the water, they removed the eggs to an incubating box, to hatch in safety.

Williams's tasks included putting radio transmitters on the adults and keeping the gulls at bay as the new hatchlings left the safety of their incubation container and headed into the surf.

Both volunteers went above and beyond their duties as well— even though they, like many, had hoped not to "get into the political stuff." They realized it was indeed a political battle, the defenseless Texas *tortugas* pitted against a major industry. Like Carole Allen, they saw no choice but to throw themselves into the fray, writing letters, speaking at hearings, and even contracting with a local pizza parlor to put educational flyers in pizza delivery boxes. Williams, a former English teacher, wrote a moving editorial for the *Corpus Christi Caller Times*, explaining that "if there were still tens of thousands of nesting Kemp's ridleys [their deaths] would be tragic but less dire. However, today so few exist that even *one* loss reduces the chances that this rare species will survive."

Mexico Sets the Standard

For all these hopeful signs, the Kemp's ridley was still not a viable species, especially not on the U.S. side of the border. Despite hype about bad environmental standards in developing countries, when it came to sea turtle protection, Mexico was putting the United States to shame. The nesting-to-stranding ratio at Padre Island National Seashore was *620 times higher* than the ratio at Rancho Nuevo. And it wasn't just the feds who were slacking: then Texas governor George W. Bush had completely ignored the situation— despite his need to score a few green points as he put in his bid for the American presidency. Under Bush the Lone Star State had been ranked by the Environmental Protection Agency and Environmental Defense Fund as the nation's top emitter of a long list of pollutants, including carbon monoxide and carbon dioxide. And the *Wall Street Journal*, in examining Bush's environmental record, pointed out his especially bad reputation among animal lovers—earned on a dove-hunting outing with reporters during which he accidentally shot a killdeer, a protected bird.

A Campaign Is Born

STRP had put Teri Shore at the helm of its Kemp's ridley efforts. As events unfolded she realized that turtle excluder devices were not going to be enough to save the Kemp's ridleys—especially given the shrimpers' aversion to them and Governor Bush's refusal to enforce their compliance. It was time to get serious about a marine reserve plan—one that barred shrimp boats from trawling the shallow waters surrounding the nesting areas on Padre Island by implementing a 20-mile-wide safety zone that would run from North to South Padre Island, where the densest concentrations of ridleys were found. Teri put together an aggressive media strategy, which began with an opinion piece by STRP's director. In the *Corpus Christi Caller Times*, Todd Steiner argued that the reserve "would offer a sanctuary for all the marine creatures within it to grow and reproduce without the pressure of commercial vessels." He added that not only would the reserve increase tourist revenues by continuing to allow recreational fishing within its borders, but commercial fisheries would also benefit from the creation of "a safe haven for shrimp and fish to grow large before migrating to open waters—where they can be captured at a more profitable size."

The groups had been advocating such a reserve for some time, but now Shore, Steiner, and Allen were in the eye of the storm. There was just one thing they were short on: money. HEART's resources were stretched as far as Allen could take them, so the San Francisco–based advocates knew they'd have to come up with the cash to take the campaign to the next level.

STRP's Peter Fugazzotto had a good idea where that money might come from. His best friend happened to be Patagonia's John Sterling, who sat on the Outdoor Industry Conservation Alliance (OICA) board. Sterling had recently told him about the Alliance and the type of environmental work it was trying to support. Sterling and Fugazzotto's relationship had already withstood long hours working together at Earth Island Institute, backpacking death marches across the Sierras, and climbing fiascos in Tuolumne Meadows. "John was my climbing instructor and a very patient one," Fugazzotto says. "He only got mad at me once because I couldn't get a piece of protection out of the rock." With such tests behind them, Fugazzotto figured he could lobby Sterling to sponsor STRP's proposal to the Conservation Alliance. Sterling, who had long been impressed by STRP's no-nonsense style and successful actions, readily agreed.

While they waited to hear from the Alliance, STRP's crew wasted no time in turning up the campaign's volume. In collaboration with Mexican environmentalist Homero Aridijis, president of the Group of 100 (Mexico's *numero uno* green group), Todd Steiner published an editorial in the *Houston Chronicle* in mid-July. The two authors asked that the United States follow in Mexico's footsteps and establish a marine reserve at Padre Island. More than 500 of the world's best-known marine scientists joined the call, and an armful of newspapers across the U.S. editorialized on the merits of a marine reserve off the shores of Texas. Because of the turtles' inability to deviate from their biologically programmed course and their need to come ashore to nest no matter what the hazards, the *Dallas Morning News* likened their slaughter to the U.S. invasion of Normandy. "Neither may deviate," the newspaper wrote. "Kemp's ridleys are compelled by nature . . . the soldiers who invaded Normandy were compelled by duty."

The Roller Coaster Ride

The good news and bad news came at once. STRP got the grant from the Conservation Alliance; it was one of the few ocean groups to receive funding from the collective of outdoor companies. The $35,000 grant was exactly what the campaign needed, and hopes soared. But before members could celebrate, the death rate of Kemp's ridleys in Texas waters leaped 42 percent—and again, the deaths were determined to be largely human caused. It was almost more than Carole Allen and the other conservationists who had worked on the Kemp's ridley issue for years could bear.

Desperate times called for desperate measures. Nothing else had worked on the Texas governor, so perhaps it was time for a little public embarrassment. Using OICA funds, STRP ran two full-page *New York Times* ads timed to ruffle feathers prior to the presidential election, for which Governor Bush had become the top Republican candidate. One ad read: IF GOVERNOR BUSH DOESN'T SAVE THE TEXAS SEA TURTLE, MAYBE PRESIDENT GORE WILL. The ad got Bush's attention; just two days after it ran, the governor authorized a deputization of seventy state game wardens to assist the feds in policing shrimpers.

The pressure was mounting on Bush and the state agencies. Thanks to the Conservation Alliance grant, STRP was also able to send its staff to Texas to work on the front lines lobbying state and federal agencies. It launched a nationwide kids' art contest. Five thousand letters from citizens flooded the State Capitol. In response to the publicity, the National Marine Fisheries Service dispatched two small "stealth" boats that could advance quickly on shrimp vessels without being detected.

As if they were beckoned by the attention, a record number of Kemp's ridleys returned to nest in southern Texas in 1999—sixteen of them all. Carole Allen and the other activists pointed to their presence, hoping to spur the government agencies to establish a reserve for them. Their response was aggravating, Allen remembers. "The Texas shrimp industry began a campaign of claiming, 'Oh, there's plenty of turtles in Mexico, so we don't need to enforce anything up here or be concerned about sea turtles in Texas waters.'"

Turning the Tide

But STRP's and HEART's public crusades were paying off. A tidal wave of resentment was rising up against Bush and his failure to act on behalf of the turtles. And the conservation community, having heard all the noise, was back on the scene. The

STRP activists demonstrate outside a Bush press event in San Francisco.

National Sierra Club, the Environmental Defense Fund, and the Center for Marine Conservation were there, as were the Audubon Council of Texas and the Caribbean Conservation Corporation. The message was a unified demand: Establish a trawl-free, sea turtle safety zone along Padre Island.

By early 2000 animal rights groups and EarthFirst! were also taking direct action: hordes of activists dressed in elaborate sea turtle costumes flooded the Texas Capitol and the World Trade Organization meeting in Seattle. The state chapters of the Sierra Club and Environmental Defense Fund held a press conference calling for the marine reserve and turtle protection. And STRP and HEART ran another full-page ad in the *New York Times*, again pointing a finger at Governor Bush for the continuing deaths of the turtles.

It was election year, and as a Republican candidate, Governor Bush was squirming. At every fund-raiser and speaking engagement he attended, he was dogged by sea turtle activists. In April the Texas Public Employees for Environmental Responsibility highlighted the governor and the sea turtles on its "Toxic Texas" Web site. And by May STRP and HEART had done such a fine job of educating the public that even the Recreational Fishing Alliance was endorsing a marine reserve.

Everyone got it but the governor and the shrimpers. And the backlash was terrible; in March thirty more turtles had washed up dead in Texas, and some with rope tied to their flippers and holes drilled through their shells. Now the conservationists were squirming, too: Were they helping or hurting the turtles if their opponents retaliated with such brutality?

STRP and the others stuck to their guns, believing that good would prevail. In May the Texas Parks and Wildlife Department proposed closing the South Texas coast to shrimp trawling as part of its revised shrimp management regulations. The action would create a safe zone out to five nautical miles from shore— a significant first step toward creating a marine reserve for the Kemp's ridleys.

On May 31 the department approved the proposal, marking the first time that a marine reserve was created with an endangered species in mind—rather than to protect the economic interests of overfished fisheries. The tide was turning in favor of the Texas *tortugas*.

After twenty years of hard work, the agencies were trying to do something significant. For people like Carole Allen, the effort seemed to have taken a lifetime. But Allen was hardly exhausted, and very grateful to the others who had come to her aid. "If the Sea Turtle Restoration Project hadn't gotten involved," she sighs, "we wouldn't be where we are now."

On August 30, 2000, the tide changed. The state of Texas announced that the South Texas coast would be closed to shrimping from December 1 through July 15; furthermore, night shrimping at any time within five nautical miles of shore was banned. The state also placed new gear restrictions on shrimp trawls, set aside more nursery areas for shrimp in the bays, and adopted federal TED laws as state regulations. Thanks to STRP's and HEART's efforts, along with those of other groups, the state of Texas received thousands of e-mails, letters, and calls during the public comment period—96 percent of them in favor of a permanent year-round closure.

Sadly, in the final days of the public comment period, the Texas Parks and Wildlife Department succumbed to the threats from the shrimp industry—otherwise the seasonal closure would have been the permanent one that citizens everywhere favored. So Carole Allen knows that the fight's not over yet; she'll need endurance and thick skin for the years to come. But for Allen, the turtles are her life's work. "I end up being a lightning rod at these public meetings," she says. "I raise the shrimpers' blood pressure and then I'm driving home alone on these dark roads, exhausted, and I'm wondering 'What am I doing? This is too much stress to handle.'" She laughs. "But you have to stay the course. You take these things on as your own."

Like a sea turtle, an activist has to stay the course. And there's something to be said for the powerful maternal instinct that allows us to take something on as our own. *Viva las tortugas,* and *viva las madres!* Where would this world be without them as our guides?

BIBLIOGRAPHY

Allen, Carole. "Groups Petition to Ban Shrimping Off Padre Island." *Padre Moon* 87 (17 September 1999).

Carr, Archie. *The Sea Turtle: So Excellent a Fishe.* Rev. ed. Austin: University of Texas Press, 1967.

Fialka, John J. "Bush, Mindful of Gore, Builds His 'Green' Credentials." *Wall Street Journal*, 13 September 1999, A46.

Phillips, Pamela. *The Great Ridley Rescue.* Missoula, Mont.: Mountain Press Publishing, 1989.

"Save the Turtles." *Dallas Morning News*, 9 August 1998, 2J.

"Sea of Change." *Dallas Morning News*, 17 May 1999, 10A.

"Sea Turtle Activists Rally for Marine Reserve." *¡Viva La Tortuga! Newsletter of the Sea Turtle Restoration Project* 1 (2000): 5.

Steiner, Todd. "Marine Reserve Is Needed for Kemp's Ridleys." *Corpus Christi Caller Times*, 24 March 1999, A9.

"Texas Sea Turtle Deaths Soar." *¡Viva La Tortuga! Newsletter of the Sea Turtle Restoration Project* 2 (1998): 4.

Tinsley, Anna M. "Dead Kemp's Ridleys on Beaches Cause Alarm." *Corpus Christi Caller Times*, 19 March 1998, A1.

"Turtles Swim Into US Presidential Race." *Marine Turtle Newsletter* 86 (October 1999): 22.

Williams, Mina G. "Sea Turtle's Plight Is Desperate." *Corpus Christi Caller Times*, 4 May 1999, A7.

"World's Sea Turtle Experts Call for Texas Marine Reserve." *¡Viva La Tortuga! Newsletter of the Sea Turtle Restoration Project* 2 (1999): 3.

The Alchemy of Democracy

The New World Mine, Outside Yellowstone
1987–1996

Earth, fire, water, air. In the Beartooth Mountains lies some of the most ancient terrain on the planet. Fiery lava was thrust upward, hardened by time, eroded by ice and wind. Only sharp stone incisors remain, the color of chocolate and smoke. Among them are glaciers and grizzlies, alpine meadows and mountain goats. Here the land seems still, but it is caught up in a seismic dance. Suddenly the range will shiver and shift—its instability can be counted on.

Water in all forms coats these mountains. The avalanches of winter rearrange boulder fields and forests in their paths. Ice splits the craggy faces of the 10,000-foot peaks, and summer rains fall in blue walls. In the spring sun, meltwater becomes a stream and moves with gravity to sustain life in the valleys below.

Yet here the 1872 Mining Law allows for another form of liquidation—that of public lands. The law is the vessel by which in 1987 Noranda, a Canadian mining conglomerate, staked a massive claim in the pure, wild soul of the Beartooths. The operation would have trickled, if not trundled, deadly waste into the headwaters of the Yellowstone River. As its machines stripped the mountains, pyrite would be exposed to air, creating a pumpkin-colored poison that could seep into streams. The chain reaction would begin: Fish would die, the bears and eagles would starve. But a handful of citizens responded to this threat by shouting a collective, thundering "No."

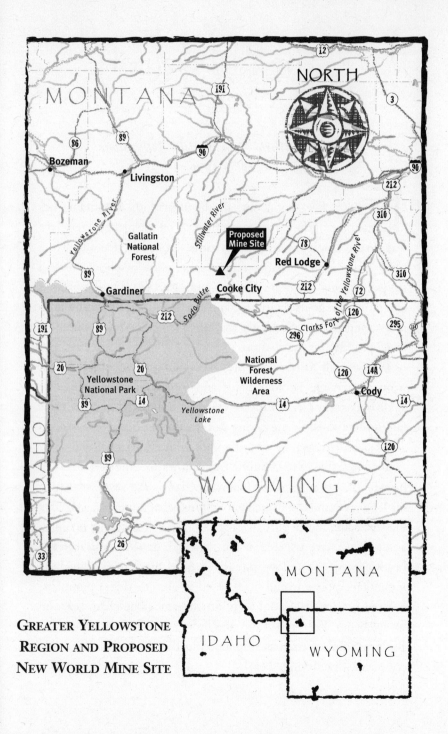

MONTANA

NORTH

Bozeman

Livingston

Gallatin
National
Forest

Yellowstone River

Stillwater River

Proposed
Mine Site

Red Lodge

Gardiner

Cooke City

Soda Butte

Clarks Fork of the Yellowstone River

Yellowstone
National Park

National
Forest
Wilderness
Area

Cody

Yellowstone
Lake

IDAHO

WYOMING

MONTANA

IDAHO

WYOMING

**GREATER YELLOWSTONE
REGION AND PROPOSED
NEW WORLD MINE SITE**

A Small Town with a Big Attitude

Certainly Noranda, Inc., didn't know who it was up against when it proposed its project in the New World Mining District. Just above Cooke City, Montana, the district stood in the doorway of the Absaroka-Beartooth Wilderness Area and less than three miles from Yellowstone National Park's northeastern boundary. The mine site itself sat on Henderson Mountain, headwaters to three tributaries of the blue-ribbon Clarks Fork of the Yellowstone River.

Perhaps Noranda thought that Cooke City folks were no match for it—after all, only seventy-five people lived there year-round. They led quiet lives, insulated by the ragged peaks of the Beartooths and the northeastern boundary of the nation's favorite national park. Or perhaps the company saw the residents as insignificant in its plans to mine Henderson—a peak that stood practically on top of Cooke City—since it never bothered to notify the locals of the changes it was about to impose on this little corner of the world. But folks in the tiny mountain town would prove to be a force to reckon with.

Take Heidi Barrett. At twenty years of age, she arrived in southern Montana in search of pure and basic mountain living. For seven years she waited tables and hoped for a chance to live permanently in Cooke City. In 1990 Heidi met a Vietnam vet named Jim. Like Heidi, he had come looking for a simple existence; when he arrived in the 1970s, he owned nothing more than his Volkswagen Beetle and an ax for chopping wood. Jim asked Heidi to the pig races over the mountain pass at the Bear Creek Saloon; the pigs they bet on won. For them it was a sign from the heavens that they were meant to be together—and together in Cooke City. They married the following year at Heidi's parents' farm in Nebraska. They roasted a pig in celebration.

The stars had indeed aligned. Heidi became Cooke City's substitute teacher and part-time postmaster, while Jim ran a carpentry business. Surrounded by millions of acres of public land, with scarcely any private land to be sold to real estate developers, Cooke City's quiet life seemed virtually guaranteed.

But in 1987 enormous trucks began trundling through town, black drill rigs perched on their backs like ravens. The rumbling rattled the town's windowpanes, wrenching the Barretts and their neighbors from their homes. Folks stood on their porches and listened to the trucks' groaning brakes and grinding gears as they turned off Highway 212 toward Daisy and Lulu Passes. Even far above them, the townspeople could still hear the trucks clawing their way toward Henderson Mountain.

Heidi started asking questions, and so did others. With the help of the Greater Yellowstone Coalition (GYC), a group based in Bozeman and dedicated to protecting the entire Yellowstone ecosystem, they discovered that Canadian-owned Noranda, through its American subsidiary, Crown Butte Mines, was about to launch a mining operation of unprecedented scale.

Mining had quite a history in Cooke City, but no one had ever struck it all that rich. In the mid-1800s everyone was looking for gold, and the fever had inflicted an exasperating cycle of boom and bust on the little town. It was a cycle the locals cared not to repeat now that recreation and tourism had concocted for them the perfect economic elixir: a steady income and a pleasant way of life.

"I never thought a mining company would seriously think about mining here again," Heidi says. "It was history as far as I was concerned, and I thought it should stay that way."

More Than Just a Mine

But the old-timers had missed the mother lode by only a few feet, and now Noranda had found it. Its plan was to extract between one and two tons of gold, silver, and copper from reserves it estimated to be worth between $600 and $800 million. The mine would draw 350 construction workers and another 175 miners, a glut of growth that Cooke City just couldn't handle. Operating twenty-four hours a day for twelve to eighteen years, the mine would send through town dozens more trucks than residents were seeing now, loaded with the guts of their beloved mountain. And of course to accommodate all the traffic and activity, a major new road and utility corridor would be carved out of prime grizzly habitat.

"We felt like we were ants getting crushed by the boots of giants," Heidi recalls. "That many miners moving into town would have changed everything."

Beartooth Alliance leaders Heidi and Jim Barrett near the site of the proposed New World project.

Worse, Noranda was planning to store the mine's waste in the Fisher Creek drainage, at the base of Henderson. There the company intended to dig out the rare alpine wetlands that served as moose breeding grounds and fill them with a plastic-lined reservoir. It was designed to hold more than five million tons of waste and would be retained at one end by a 100-foot earthen dam. When the mining operation was completed, the reservoir's water level would be dropped and the tailings or waste byproducts then suffocated with rock and cement, so that no air could mix with the tailings to generate sulfuric acid—the death knell to nearby water sources if it leaked. Crown Butte's engineers promised that the sulfuric acid produced prior to the pond being plugged would never leach into the water sources. They called their plans "state of the art," although they had never actually been tried before in a high-mountain setting.

"State of the art," scoffs Heidi Barrett. She may have been a farm girl from Nebraska, but she knew better than to believe that an oversized plastic kiddie pool could withstand an eternity of high-alpine realities like avalanches, flooding, freeze-thaw cycles, and earthquakes. And when the thing finally gave, it would drain its heavy metals right into the Clarks Fork, just over the state line—Wyoming's one and only Wild and Scenic River. The Clarks Fork is a major tributary of the Yellowstone River—the life source for Yellowstone Park.

Citizens Unite

Heidi wasn't the only one crying foul. By now the entire town was in a tizzy over the passing trucks and the dark future they carried on their skids. At a town meeting held at the fire station, a majority of locals decided that they wanted to fight the mine—and to come out with their guns blazing. Hardly anything was worth risking the peace and stability of their little town, and nothing imaginable was worth wounding the world of Yellowstone.

The citizens named themselves the Beartooth Alliance, after the pointed peaks that fortressed their home. Between themselves and seasonal residents, they signed up seventy-five members.

But these folks were fishing guides, bartenders, general-store operators. They didn't have a clue how to fight a multimillion-dollar international corporation, and so far the Forest Service had been of no help to them—even though public lands in its care would be affected by the operation. The federal agency, which managed most of the Beartooths, swore there was nothing it could do, thanks to the archaic Mining Law of 1872.

The Miner's Favorite Law

This law had been passed in a fit of legislative shortsightedness, ironically in the same year that Congress had also had the vision to establish Yellowstone as the first national park preserve anywhere in the world. Enacted to promote westward expansion, the 1872 law allowed prospectors to stake a claim on public land and buy it for no more than five dollars an acre. Once a claim was made, mining that piece of public real estate took precedence over any other land uses. Thanks to a powerful mining lobby, the law has hardly changed since its inception. Today mining companies still don't pay a penny in royalties—although oil and gas corporations must—and the government still cannot reject a claim if it is legally "valid," regardless of the environmental threats. The way the law reads, the government can take action against a company only retroactively—after the damage is done. What's more, in what must be the best real estate deal of the last two centuries, the mining company essentially becomes the owner of this once-public land. It can turn around and sell its patented claim for any asking price it can get, or it can develop the land in any way it sees fit. Heidi shuddered to think that, after the New World Mine project was completed, Noranda could sell "its" property to some ambitious developer who would drop a ski area or a subdivision on it. Such gross human intrusion would forever fracture a wide, wild place that imperiled species like the grizzly bear and wolf needed for survival.

The Noranda mine was patented, or essentially bought, for only $225. But the company was going to extract millions from Henderson's volcanic beds high in the Montana mountains. And there was no guarantee that it would clean up properly afterward. Mining companies in the West have a long history of leaving a trail of tears—of poisoned water and soil, garish road scars, and naked, eroding hillsides. Before the government can tell them to clean up their acts, the companies file bankruptcy and walk away—the profits protected by some subsidiary obscured in a corporate maze. If history is a good yardstick, folks could anticipate that the taxpayers would get stuck with the cleanup bill for Noranda, too. Besides, Noranda's track record wasn't so hot. A *U.S. News and World Report* investigation found that of Noranda's six mining exploration operations, four were in court for pollution violations and two were potential Superfund sites.

Despite all this, the Forest Service threw up its hands and said it was helpless to do anything. But GYC, in its seventeen years of working to protect the Yellowstone ecosystem as a whole, had heard this tune before from the federal land management agencies. The group was unflustered by it, and told the Beartooth Alliance to hang tough.

Citizen Alchemy

So an intense amalgamation of tactics began. Jim and Heidi went to Billings, where the Northern Plains Resource Council taught them about grassroots organizing while GYC put its scientists and legal watchdogs to work sniffing around the skirts of the mother lode. For the next several years, the groups worked together, stockpiling information to be used as ammunition against Noranda. GYC built court cases around Clean Water Act violations, the project's Achilles' heel, and challenged every new permit that Noranda filed, which caused the company a frustrating series of delays. Meanwhile, the Beartooth Alliance hit the ground running. Members decided that one of their first priorities was to collect samples from the various water sources that could be affected by the mine. The samples would be used in a before-and-after baseline comparison with the samples offered up by Noranda to comply with environmental regulations. So Cooke City residents informed the Forest Service of their intentions and signed with them a memorandum of understanding for the future comparison. On their days off folks took to the hills on snowshoes or skis, climbing every ridge and descending every drainage until they were certain they had vials of water from every potential leaching site.

Jim Barrett, Heidi's husband, was a guy with a keen sense of civic responsibility. In his early days in Cooke City, he'd even served as the town sheriff for two years. He patrolled in his VW Bug, a cherry-red light on its top the only signal of his authority. The most trouble he usually faced was an occasional brawl in the local tavern. Begrudgingly he'd break it up, only to walk outside and find that the barflies had gotten even by turning his car on its side in the parking lot.

But this was a new kind of trouble, and not the kind that a sheriff's badge could resolve. So Jim cut back on his carpentry commitments and with his wife plunged headfirst into the Beartooth Alliance. They began conducting nightly slide shows for tourists passing through on their way to Yellowstone and set up a countywide campaign to implement zoning ordinances—aimed at making it difficult for Noranda to house its mass of miners.

While the Beartooth Alliance could operate on a shoestring, concocting local-citizen actions from their kitchen tables, GYC needed resources for the big-picture fight: media advertising, lawsuits, lobbying, research, and educational materials. Recognizing what was at stake for the waters and wildlife of Yellowstone, it was easy for GYC's board to commit any and all funds to stopping Noranda's New World Mine. Late in 1993 the serious hunt for money began.

Business Backing

Patagonia, the clothing company made famous by its iron-forged climbing pitons, was already actively supporting the Greater Yellowstone Coalition's efforts to stop the mine. Through its environmental "tithing" program, it was funding a GYC volunteer who was on the road making public presentations about the Noranda mine and the threat it posed. On a day when the coffers were looking especially empty, Mike Clark, GYC's executive director, called Patagonia's Jil Zilligen to ask if she knew of other funding sources he could pursue. She immediately suggested the Outdoor Industry Conservation Alliance (OICA), of which Patagonia was a member. Given the nature of the project and its urgency, she thought that it might mesh nicely with the OICA's funding principles. Mike and his staff crafted a proposal and fired it off, fingers crossed.

Jil remembers well the board meeting in which the Conservation Alliance voted on the "Mine from Hell" campaign. The OICA was outraged by the mine and very much in favor of GYC's strategy for stopping it. "Their proposal far and away cleared the ranks. It got an unbelievable amount of votes," she says.

A check for $30,000 dollars was cut to GYC. It was spontaneous combustion: The little Cooke City campaign went national.

Mike Clark, a well-seasoned environmental advocate, felt that a national campaign made perfect sense. The Noranda mine threatened one of the nation's most beloved landscapes, and Mike knew most Americans would be appalled. "One-third of all Americans will visit Yellowstone Park in their lifetime," he says. "It's a pilgrimage for most of us. That's why the money and enthusiasm of the Conservation Alliance was so significant: It allowed us to take the problem to the American people."

Mike was right. As GYC members began contacting national media, the response was overwhelmingly sympathetic to their cause. "We took hundreds of reporters to the mine site," Mike recalls. "Of all the big press we got, in publications like *Time, U.S. News and World Report*, and the *Washington Post*, only one article was ever in favor of the mine—and that came from the *Toronto News*, out of Noranda's hometown."

By this time numerous other environmental groups were pitching in where they were needed, and a New Mexico congressman had introduced legislation to protect the mine site as a National Recreation Area. With funds in the bank and so much help from others, GYC now had the ability to go snooping—and find out who the mine's friends and investors were. The individuals identified were then sent information on the grave threats that the mine posed, and company bigwigs were cornered at cocktail parties and embarrassed by the mess they were making on Yellowstone's doorstep.

Citizens come out in full force for a Crown Butte presentation on the New World Mine.

Various businesses were on board, too. Not only had Patagonia begun a campaign in its stores across the country, but a local clothing manufacturer, Wyoming Woolens, had also leaped into the fray. The company was owned and operated by Frannie Huff, who'd started out by sewing men's woolen shirts in her living room. Frannie had long appreciated small towns and pristine western landscapes—she'd moved to Wyoming right out of high school for just these reasons. Why anyone would mess with the Yellowstone ecoregion—the wild soul of America—was beyond her. So when Frannie purchased her first delivery truck to get her goods to retailers throughout the intermountain West, she decided to put it on the road with a message. STOP THE NEW WORLD

MINE! its panels blazed. Wyoming Woolens' success grew as the campaign escalated. When Frannie opened her own retail store in Jackson, she aired GYC-produced videos and encouraged customers to pen postcards to elected officials, asking them to save Yellowstone. She even paid for the stamps.

Corporate Intimidation

By now GYC and the Beartooth Alliance had an entire cauldron of tactics brewing, and Noranda officials were sweating. But three factors were preventing the groups from making progress against the mine. First, Congress apparently wasn't in the mood to protect national treasures at the time, so the bill to designate the mine site as a National Recreation Area wasn't getting much traction. Second, the company still was protected legally by the mining law of yesteryear. Finally, although Noranda's Toronto honchos were meeting graciously with GYC, the company's more impassioned local representatives were bullying citizens of Cooke City.

"The mining company tried very hard to intimidate us," Heidi Barrett recalls. "First they sent out an unidentified and ambiguous letter to residents, insinuating that they were county commissioners who thought that the zoning plan we had successfully petitioned was not in the best interests of the community." The letter confused many folks, who then rescinded their petition signatures by mailing in a postcard provided by Noranda. Heidi adds, "When we researched the letter's origin, we discovered the return address was linked to a mine official. We had to go back, reeducate the community, and start all over gathering the 60 percent of the district's landowners' signatures required to submit the petition." Noranda then told the Beartooth Alliance that if it pursued the zoning issue, the company would sue. "Some folks were about to pee their pants, they were so scared," says Heidi. "But we convinced everyone to hang tight, and fortunately the corporation never made good on its threat."

There were other problems. The mining company's local representatives made strong economic arguments pointing up the dollars that new miners-in-residence would add to townspeople's pockets. The folks who agreed turned on Beartooth Alliance members, and things in town got a bit tense. The original chairman of the alliance was a man named Wade King, who lived in a trailer for which he paid $150 a month in rent. Noranda reps approached his landlord and said that they would pay $600 a month; the landlord told Wade to match that amount or get out. Forced to live in a tent, Wade continued his work for the citizens' group—and continued to be harassed. He was even beat up in the local bar by a mining proponent; ironically, the bar's name had just been changed to the Miner's Saloon—in the hope of cashing in from the people who would soon be gutting Henderson Mountain.

Even Heidi and Jim had trouble. Jim was a runner in his spare time. One day a friend of the couple who worked in a local diner overheard a local in favor of the mine say that "next time he saw that Jim Barrett out running, he'd 'door' him with his pickup and break both his legs." Heidi, who had occasionally used the fax machine at the Sinclair gas station for Beartooth business, was greeted by a fax bill charging her $9.00 per page. Apparently the station owner had been tempted by the prospect of fueling the Noranda crowd's trucks.

Then came the real kicker. Jim had taken over as chairman of the alliance while Heidi became its sole staff person, committed full time to its membership recruitment and administrative duties. In 1995 the Forest Service called the Barretts and said that it would need the citizens' water samples, because Noranda had decided there was no need to waste company time and money collecting new ones when samples were already available. Heidi and Jim refused to part with the samples, saying that they were paid for and owned by the citizens of the Beartooth Alliance. After all, the whole point of collecting the samples was to compare them with Noranda's. Regardless, the Forest Service sent representatives to the Beartooth Alliance office to demand that the equipment be turned over immediately. Heidi, who was alone at the time, locked the door and told them to go away. A federal marshal was called to confiscate the water sampling equipment, and he was not nearly as easygoing as Jim had been as sheriff. The samples were turned over to the feds and eventually to Noranda.

Heidi was dismayed. "Through the mine fight I realized that the agencies that we as citizens trust to do the right thing for the land are actually often on the side of industry and corporations. As a child, the Forest Service meant Smokey the Bear, a benevolent creature. As an adult, I find that he is having dinner with the mine's officials and thinks it's a great thing to put a large industrial complex in a remote, beautiful part of the National Forest."

Defiance Pays Off

But despite the aggravations, neither the Barretts nor the Beartooth citizens caved. They continued their nightly slide shows for tourists and took turns driving to the park to spread the word among visitors. Heidi continued to organize tours of the mine site for officials and journalists. And outside Cooke City the racket they were making was beginning to pay off. The new superintendent of Yellowstone, Mike Finley, had taken an aggressive stance against the mine, and eventually asked the question, "How could the logical mind approve this?" The *New York Times* also took a bullish posture; on August 29, 1994, its op ed page commented, "The company says it can pull eight million tons of ore out of the mountain, fill a 77-acre lake 10 stories deep with waste and seal it for eternity. That sort of technological confidence chills the blood."

The *Times* editorial, the first in a series that won a Pulitzer Prize, called the White House on the carpet for its inaction. The piece declared that "if people like Secretary of the Interior Bruce Babbitt and Vice President Al Gore genuinely wish to be remembered as aggressive and caring stewards for the country's environment, they will quickly seek ways to stop this threat in its tracks."

Pointing to a century of "unregulated mining [that] has left behind 500,000 abandoned mines, 50 billion tons of waste and 10,000 miles of dead streams," the *Times* went on to say in another opinion that "if the E.P.A. [Environmental Protection Agency] cannot weigh in on a project like this one, then it has no reason to exist."

Finally, in August 1995, tired of the administration's inaction, the *Times* printed the suggestion that President Clinton take a quick helicopter flight from the ranch in the Tetons where he was vacationing to the New World Mine site. It reminded the president that, at a recent town meeting in Billings, he had told Sue Glidden, co-owner of the Cooke City General Store, that he was "very worried" about the mine. "The way things look now," wrote America's most influential paper, "the agencies are likely to give Noranda the go-ahead in exchange for pledges that the company will spend whatever is required to prevent environmental damage." The paper claimed that such a decision simply would not be good enough. "Even if the company takes extraordinary precautions every step of the way, it cannot guarantee that the poisons produced now can be safely contained for future generations."

Jaws dropped across the nation. Between the media blitz inspired by GYC and the grassroots efforts of the Beartooth Alliance and Conservation Alliance businesses, letters inundated the White House, begging the Clinton administration to do something about the foreign corporation that was poised to pillage their best national treasure. "The White House received more mail on the New World Mine than any other issue that year," Mike Clark observes. Even Senator Craig Thomas, a Republican from Wyoming who usually sided with industry, announced publicly that "there is only so long you can withhold your opinion when in fact you have a strong conviction that this might be the worst place to site a mine."

Finally President Clinton got the hint. After touring the mine site, he announced a mining moratorium on the Forest Service lands that surrounded the Noranda claims. Sadly, it was a gesture without many teeth, since by law Noranda still had the right to mine its claims. But the delays that GYC was creating via the permitting process and its litigation, the public attention drawn to the operation by Cooke City citizens, and the president's action all sent a strong signal that America was intent on protecting its most cerished national park.

Protesters at a clean water rally in Billings.

At the Table

At this point, not only was the administration sheepish about the public's response to its inaction on Noranda, but two of the company's owners, Edward and Peter Broffman, were outright embarrassed by the bad press and the mailings that their friends and investors were receiving on their mining operation. Both were generous philanthropists and committed to many civic affairs, figuring prominently in both Canadian and international social circles. Publicly humiliated and their confidence shaken by the recent events, the Broffman brothers eagerly accepted GYC's offer to visit Noranda's Toronto headquarters in December 1995.

GYC's message was loud and clear: Noranda couldn't win because the coalition would fight it forever. Noranda took this promise to heart, since GYC's series of legal actions was in fact succeeding against the company. But GYC told Noranda that there was a way out. Mike Clark and four GYC board members offered to represent Noranda and work out a deal with the administration so the company would receive compensation for the resources it had expended on the mine—in exchange for giving up the prospect of any further activity at the New World site.

"At first we weren't sure if they were being straight with us— since my experience with the American mining companies is that they are never honest," Mike says. But in the end he walked out the door with a letter authorizing GYC to broker a deal with the White House on Noranda's behalf. So the negotiations began. Over the next six months, the Greater Yellowstone Coalition met with a special committee chaired by Vice President Al Gore himself. The talks, which included heavy hitters like the EPA's Carol Browner, seemed to move forward in geologic time, with every round miring the stakeholders in technicalities. Toward the end there were mind-racking all-night sessions. It was a grueling time for Mike Clark and the others.

Finally, in 1996, a deal was forged. The New World Agreement stated that the federal government would trade $65 million in less ecologically significant public lands and other assets for the company's agreement to suspend all permitting activities for the proposed mine. As icing on the cake, Noranda committed itself to place more than $22 million in an escrow account to be used to clean up existing pollution at the site. It was an elemental victory for the Greater Yellowstone region and Americans everywhere.

The GYC folks flew back to Montana, at once exhausted and elated. But there were no reprieves for the weary: The administration contacted Mike the next morning, saying that the president would be at the mine site in just twenty-four hours to announce the agreement. Everyone involved scrambled to get out of work or arrange for baby-sitters so they could attend the event.

A High-Altitude Victory

The next day two hundred citizens from Cooke City and the surrounding areas stood at the base of Baronett Peak. They watched a fleet of helicopters approach, circle like eagles, then deposit the president and his staff members on the high ground of their home turf. "It was such an emotional moment for all of us," Mike Clark remembers. "There we were next to the president, signing this document in front of all the folks that had worked so hard to see this day. It was a great example of democracy in action, how citizens can get involved in their own backyard and even get the president of the United States to join them there."

The Budweiser flowed in Cooke City that night as everyone gathered to celebrate their hard-won victory. It was a night of reflection—and redirection for some. The Beartooth Alliance's work was finished, but Heidi Barrett had gained a deep love for environmental advocacy. Both she and Jim were psychically drained after fighting Noranda for nearly seven years straight, often seven days a week. Besides, they had a three-year-old son in need of time with other kids his age. So when a position came open at GYC's office in Bozeman as 1997 wrapped up, Heidi applied. Now working in fund-raising development for the coalition, Heidi says that "protecting the Greater Yellowstone ecosystem seems second nature to me. I will fight always for this special place." Jim feels much the same way. He moved on to become the executive director of the Park County Environmental Council in Livingston, Montana, a citizens' group working to protect the county's natural resources from industrialization.

Frannie Huff now serves GYC, too, as a board member. She reflects with pride on the campaign that stopped the New World Mine. "At the time GYC was a small group, and they were spending a lot of their reserves to fight Noranda. The money from the Conservation Alliance really helped them at a crucial time during a crucial battle. I really applaud the Conservation Alliance for such efforts; it's made such a difference. If all businesses committed to actions in their backyards, the world would take care of itself."

It was the sweetest, most potent kind of environmental victory: one fought and won by grassroots forces fueled by conscientious businesses.

Mike Clark recently told the *High Country News* that "the Yellowstone is one of the very few landscapes left that Lewis and Clark might actually recognize." Indeed, the Greater Yellowstone region remains the true gold of the West—as it was centuries ago—despite our misguided attempts at its transmutation. The Beartooths, the stately stewards of Yellowstone headwaters, long ago emerged from some of the oldest stone and soil on earth. They now offer us an array of clues about the origins of our planet and even our solar system—the keys to the great alchemic mystery of our beginnings. "Geologically, the Beartooth Mountains make up one of the most amazing places in the U.S.," Mike Clark says. "A lot of powerful forces come together there."

BIBLIOGRAPHY

Anderson, Bob. *Beartooth Country: Montana's Absaroka and Beartooth Mountains.* Helena, Mont.: Unicorn Publishing, 1994.

"Blocking the Yellowstone Mine" (editorial). *New York Times*, 18 September 1994.

"Cancelling the New World Mine" (editorial). *New York Times*, 10 December 1995.

Dawson, Patrick, and John Skow. "Mother Lode vs. Mother Nature: Archaic U.S. Mining Laws Could Let a Canadian Gold Rush Threaten Yellowstone National Park." *Time*, 22 November 1993, 58.

DiSilvestro, Roger. "Is This a Bad Deal for Taxpayers?" *National Wildlife*, 20 October 1997, 36.

Ekey, Bob. "The New World Agreement: A Call for Reform of the 1872 Mining Law." *Public Land & Resources Law Review* 18 (1997).

"Environmental Ups and Downs: A Sad Death for Mining Law Reform" (editorial). *New York Times*, 3 October 1994.

Kesselheim, Alan S. "The Last Wild River." *High Country News*, 27 March 2000, 1–11.

McManus, Reed. "New World, Old Story." *Sierra*, 1 September 1994, 88.

Miller, Ken. "Bill Would Put Yellowstone Area Off Proposed Mine." Gannett News Service, 14 June 1995.

"Mr. Clinton Acts on Yellowstone" (editorial). *New York Times*, 29 August 1995.

"Mr. Clinton Can Save Yellowstone" (editorial). *New York Times*, 14 August 1995.

"No Mines Near Yellowstone" (editorial). *New York Times*, 29 August 1994.

Satchell, Michael. "A New Battle Over Yellowstone Park." *U.S. News and World Report*, 13 March 1995, 34–42.

"Stopping the Yellowstone Mine" (editorial). *New York Times*, 27 March 1995.

The New Vertical Adventure

The Clavey River, California
1990–1996

Conrad Anker's biggest accomplishment may not be finding the facedown, frozen body of George Mallory on Mount Everest in 1999—a discovery that enlightened the debate about who really first set foot on the world's highest summit. Nor may his biggest achievement be some of the world's most difficult ascents: Kalldaha Spire in the Indian Himalayas, the Streaked Wall in Utah's Zion, and Mount Craddock, Antarctica's third tallest peak. Yes, the thirty-something Californian has carried stranded climbers down mountains and survived for a week without food in an icebound tent. And he has endured the untimely, tragic deaths of countless climbing partners who were also dear friends—some of the greatest American climbers, including Alex Lowe, Mugs Stump, and Seth Shaw.

In fact, Conrad's most significant contribution to the world won't be found among the pages of the *American Alpine Journal* or *Climbing* magazine. Instead it will be found in the enduring life story of rare bats, wild grapes, rainbow trout, and Yosemite National Park's deer herd—whose winter forage depends upon a single river, which this great alpinist and dozens of other citizens joined to save.

Greater Yosemite Be Dammed

Conrad, and two generations of Ankers before him, make up just one of the many stories that took place to save the Clavey River, the last free-flowing river in Tuolumne County—Conrad's home

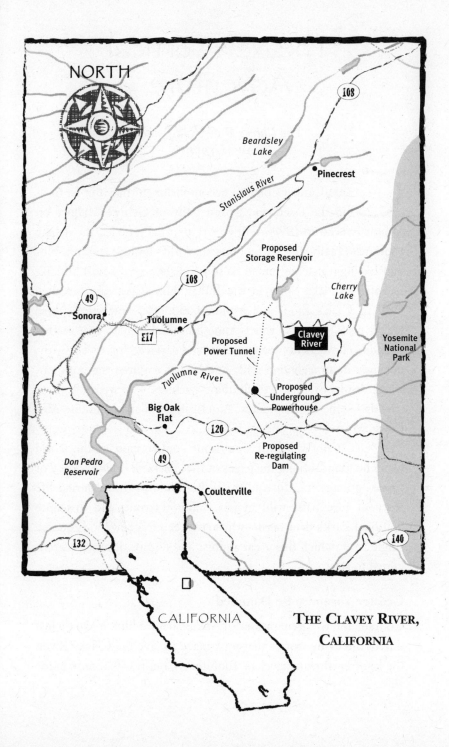

NORTH

108

Beardsley Lake

● Pinecrest

Stanislaus River

Proposed
Storage Reservoir

Cherry Lake

108

49

Sonora ●

Tuolumne ●

E17

Proposed
Power Tunnel

Clavey
River

Yosemite
National
Park

Tuolumne River

Proposed
Underground
Powerhouse

Big Oak
Flat ●

120

Proposed
Re-regulating
Dam

49

*Don Pedro
Reservoir*

● Coulterville

132

140

CALIFORNIA

**THE CLAVEY RIVER,
CALIFORNIA**

turf in the central Sierras. The fight was as daunting as any stone face; saving the Clavey from a $707 million hydropower project meant stopping a 413-foot dam that would have flooded 655 acres and inundated 3 miles of the river corridor. It also meant halting 11,000 feet of pipeline, an 11-mile tunnel, transmission lines, a powerhouse, and 30 miles of construction roads. And it meant going up against a mountain of power and bureaucracy—from powerful water interests to a public land management agency that catered to business interests far more than it did the public.

The Clavey was one of the last four undammed rivers in the entire Sierra Nevadas and its destruction would forever alter the Greater Yosemite area, through which it flowed. Wandering for 47 miles from its headwaters in the Emigrant Wilderness through the Stanislaus National Forest just west of Yosemite National Park, the river and its corridor may comprise the last fully intact aquatic ecosystem in the region. And its qualities are extraordinary: In 1971 the California Department of Fish and Game designated the Clavey a Wild Trout Stream, to recognize its thriving native trout population—one entirely undiluted by stocked fish and revered by anglers everywhere. The watershed also harbors the forest's largest remaining stand of quaking aspen as well as twelve plant and animal candidates for listing as threatened or endangered. At its confluence with the Wild and Scenic Tuolumne, the river surges into the thundering Clavey Falls, a highlight of the hundreds of commercial and private raft trips that pass by. And the Clavey itself is a challenging technical, Class V boating adventure.

"Mountains, unless they're strip-mined off the top, don't have the sense of immediate and complete devastation that a ruined river does," Conrad would say later. He couldn't have been more accurate.

The free-flowing Clavey River at 6,000 feet elevation near the Emigrant Wilderness.

A Family Affair

Protecting the Clavey was a community affair—and for some a family one as well. The Ankers were into their fifth generation in the central Sierras; since 1853 they had owned and operated a ranch near a tiny town with the deceptive name of Big Oak Flat. It was a wonderful place to call home; the charming community was surrounded by the great gray walls of Yosemite, the high-alpine country of Tuolumne, and the rolling, golden hills of oak that are quintessential northern California. After a stint in many of the world's urban centers—where he was employed first as a serviceman and then as a banker—Conrad's father, Wally, returned to the area with an East German bride named Helga.

"My mom and dad used to fish the Clavey all the time," Wally remembers. "So it's always been a part of our history. I remember the Clavey in the 1940s—it was wild and impressive and hard to get to. Then when I left and found myself living in big cities, I realized in a broader sense how important, how rare, such a place is."

Settled back in Big Oak Flat, it was this sentiment that drew Wally through the doorway of a local Sierra Club chapter meeting. Soon Wally found himself as chair of the chapter. But when the Clavey River dam was proposed, Wally and others sensed that the club might not be the best group to lead the opposition—the chapter had tried to prevent a dam on the nearby Stanislaus River but was defeated. The dam went up largely because the chapter's campaign wasn't portrayed as having local support—dam advocates made it clear to media and decision makers that only city slickers and weekend rafters opposed the project. And since the Sierra Club was considered "too radical" for a lot of locals, the group recognized that a diverse, community-based coalition, joined with the expertise and resources of the Tuolumne River Preservation Trust (TRPT), would have to carry the Clavey campaign.

Two Groups Are Better than One

TRPT had been formed in 1981 to save the Tuolumne River from a billion-dollar dam project proposed by Turlock and Modesto Irrigation Districts. After a long battle on the floor of Congress, an 83-mile stretch of the river was listed under the federal Wild and Scenic Rivers Act, effectively halting the dam project and protecting the river in its free state for future generations. In 1990 the trust turned its attention to the Clavey. By intervening in Turlock Irrigation District's (TID) application process to the Federal Energy Regulatory Commission (FERC), it forced the agency to look long and hard at the applicant's environmental impact studies. The proposed Clavey River hydroproject was massaged out of an eleventh-hour compromise brokered among citizens and politicians as part of the bill for the Tuolumne's Wild and Scenic designation. In what the dam developers interpreted to be an "unwritten" understanding in the legislation, tributaries of the Tuolumne were considered by them to be open to future development. Although the bill's language said that the Wild and Scenic designation of the Tuolumne wouldn't "preclude" development on the smaller waters that fed it, river advocates protested that the words did not automatically approve future dams.

The Clavey River Preservation Coalition (CRPC) board of directors was forged from every niche in the community—a rancher, schoolteachers, hotel and restaurant owners, an archaeologist, biologists, river outfitters and guides, carpenters, fly anglers, and llama breeders—all gathered together to do the volunteer work of the citizen coalition. Together, the CRPC and the Tuolumne River Preservation Trust set out to stop Turlock again—and they knew Wild and Scenic designation would once more do the trick. The two groups appealed to the chief of the Forest Service a 1991 Stanislaus National Forest Service decision, which found the Clavey "eligible" for Wild and Scenic status, but "not suitable." The agency's own biologists found fifteen "outstandingly remarkable values" on the river. Forest Service officials explained that if not for Turlock's dam proposal, they would have recommended the Clavey for protection.

A Haunting Legacy

At this point, fighting hydro projects was nothing new to Tuolumne County. The residents saw every day the drowned Hetch Hetchy Valley, where the wild, roaring waters of the upper Tuolumne River had been tamed to stillness and silence behind an immense concrete wall. In the early 1900s Hetch Hetchy had been a brutal battle, with the city of San Francisco pitted against wilderness visionary John Muir, who in his book *The Yosemite* called Hetch Hetchy Valley "one of Nature's rarest and most precious mountain temples." As the dam proposal inched forward, with its advocates arguing that the Bay Area desperately needed the water supply, Muir blasted the project in an unpublished journal, writing:

> *A great political miracle this of "improving" the beauty of the most beautiful of all mountain parks by cutting down its groves, and burying all the thicket of azalea and wild rose, lily gardens, and ferneries two or three hundred feet deep. After this is done we are promised a road blasted on the slope of the north wall, where nature-lovers may sit on rustic stools, or rocks, like frogs on logs, to admire the sham dam lake, the grave of Hetch Hetchy.*

Some folks in Tuolumne County may have been a bit gun-shy of greens—especially after all the nasty timber wars up north—but they were protective of the lands around their homes and couldn't bear to see another Hetch Hetchy disaster. And they knew that a county for which tourism—spawned largely by the nearby rivers—was an important source of revenue, blocking those revenue streams just didn't make economic sense. Whether they liked it or not, a majority of the residents were about to become environmental activists.

New Constituents Through a New Campaign

As for TRPT, it had tackled what was perhaps the most crucial component of the effort to protect the Clavey. The Turlock Irrigation District's Rate-Payer's Campaign exposed to users of Turlock electricity just how poorly the economics of the dam project stacked up. With the expert testimony of an energy economist and a representative from Bay Area Utilities District both condemning the project, the two groups attracted some unlikely allies—the Tuolumne County Farm Bureau and Butterball Turkey were hardly the kind of entities that environmental groups were used to siding with. Bob Hackamack, a chemical engineer who sat on the energy subcommittee of TRPT, testified that "if that project were in place today, Turlock's rates would have to jump 20 percent to cover it." The rate hike was bad news, considering that the county's big industry was leaving the area, complaining that Turlock's electric rates had already risen 17 percent in the past two years.

With the success of the outreach to energy rate payers, resulting in support from more than just the usual suspects, the fight to save the Clavey became much more than an environmental issue. Indeed, this was the turning point for the entire campaign.

Such was the opposition stacked up against John Mills, the water district's project manager. Undaunted, John charged ahead with Turlock's application to dam the Clavey, refusing to look at alternatives that TRPT's experts had found would be two to four times cheaper, with quicker implementation and far less degradation to the environment. But this was a power company whose multimillion-dollar annual budget allocated only $35 a year for energy-conserving measures. Supported by Friends of the River and several other groups, the Tuolumne River Preservation Trust and the citizens' coalition weren't about to let developers again make the same mistake on a central Sierra river, especially a Tuolumne tributary in such wild and pristine condition. The mission was simple: to stop the dam, but also to obtain federal Wild and Scenic status so future dam proposals wouldn't threaten the Clavey. But however simple, the fight was going to be expensive.

Grassroots Fund-raising

After gaining protection for the Tuolumne, TRPT was seasoned in fund-raising, and under the auspices of a dedicated board and the group's executive director, Johanna Thomas, they raised over $500,000 during the seven-year campaign. Donations came from many sources. Tuolumne river outfitters, although not exactly millionaires, had every year since the early 1980s made a contribution to TRPT based on the number of folks they took down the river each day. As longtime TRPT board member Joe Daly says, "This type of dedicated backing in order to save the Clavey and Tuolumne assisted the trust through some of its leanest financial winters."

Other outdoor businesses contributed by way of a grant from the Outdoor Industry Conservation Alliance (OICA). The grant proposal was sponsored by Patagonia—largely because the staff members in its San Francisco store, led by veteran Patagoniac Ron Hunter, were so committed to TRPT and saving the Clavey. In fact, not only did the store dedicate a wall to an informational display about the imperiled river, but its employees ran a letter-writing campaign on the issue for nearly a year.

Given TRPT's track record—with 83 miles of protected, wild, and free Tuolumne under its belt—the Alliance gave a quick and easy vote of confidence, trusting that the group could stop yet another central Sierra dam. A check for $30,000 was delivered to TRPT and, combined with the other incoming resources, the campaign avalanched.

The Power of the People

TRPT and CRPC hit Tuolumne County dirt running, reaching out to business owners and residents from every walk of life. Public hearings were scheduled, and the groups made sure that advocates of the river were heard loud and clear. Jim Krenzel, a representative of Highway 120 Association, a business owners' group, reminded the Forest Service and other agencies that "fully one-third of those tourists that we service . . . are rafters. . . . [The dam] will greatly impact the business in that corridor." Don Moyer, a longtime angler and fishing writer, spoke to the amount of water the project proposed removing from the river—which was nearly 90 percent. He pointed out that this would leave the river running at two cubic feet per second. "Gosh," he said. "I've

TRPT activists monitor a meadow in the Clavey River's watershed.

seen more water than that running down the street in a good rainstorm!" Conrad's grandmother, Margaret Anker, also spoke. "We now have many dams in Tuolumne County. We only have one free-flowing river left. The Clavey." Despite her ninety years, her voice rang with strength and clarity. People in the audience cheered. Conrad beams with pride at this memory of his grandmother. "You know," he laughs, "had my grandfather been alive, she probably wouldn't have been allowed to testify. Even though he loved the outdoors, he was really from that older generation of thinking that all industrial progress was good—even dams."

The results of TRPT's and CRPC's efforts were impressive. By late summer in 1994, the Federal Energy Regulatory Commission came out against licensing the Clavey River Project, saying that there was insufficient "public benefit" to justify the wide range of negative environmental consequences—including damage to the native trout fishery, special-status wildlife, old-growth forest, riparian habitats, and the river basin's primitive character. For FERC to denounce a dam project on environmental grounds was unheard of, and sent a clear message to Turlock Irrigation that the project was already off track. Still, Turlock refused to throw in the towel.

There had been some headway made on the legislative front, with Congressman George Miller and Senator Barbara Boxer poised to run with a Wild and Scenic bill in both the House and Senate. But the 1994 congressional election ushered in Newt Gingrich and company, and the congressional mood soured on environmental legislation. Both legislators remained cheerleaders for the Clavey, with the senator even attending a CRPC fundraiser in Big Oak Flat, but they said there was no point in even trying to introduce a bill until Congress changed again.

TRPT and the citizens' coalition were also able to run some hard-hitting, full-page ads in the *Turlock Journal*. One began with a question conceived by TRPT's Johanna Thomas: "What do a rainbow trout and your wallet have in common?" The answer: "They'll both get picked clean by TID's Clavey Dam Project." The two groups floated politicians and journalists down the river, and the Sierra Club joined them to host a weeklong activist training program that included hiking and rafting in the river corridor, and educational campfire talks with naturalists and representatives of the Me-Wuk Tribal Council—who had signed on in opposition to the dam.

On March 1, 1995, the Turlock Irrigation District notified the Federal Energy Regulatory Commission that it was pulling its license application for the Clavey River project. The excuse given by company officials was a "downturn in the state's economy."

A "Suitable" River

It was a sweet summit for the groups to have reached, and they liked the view. But as with any big mountain, getting to the top is only half the effort—you're not safe until you've made it back down as well. CRPC had some Conservation Alliance funds left in the bank, and it still had to convince the Forest Service to recommend the Clavey River as "suitable" for Wild and Scenic status. Without the support of the agency that managed the Clavey watershed, there was little chance that Congress would ever give it the enduring protection it needed from future dam proposals and other projects.

Little did Wally Anker realize that additional funds would come by way of his own son. After all, Conrad lived the "dirt-bag" life of a climber—with few possessions save a climbing rack and a lot of rope. But serendipity prevailed. Wally, who had always been intensely involved in his children's lives, decided to tag along with Conrad to a company meeting of The North Face (TNF), the outdoor company that sponsored his climbing ventures. Bill Simon, who was president of TNF at the time, spoke to his employees, describing the company's new role as a member of the Conservation Alliance of the outdoor industry. He said the Alliance was looking for a worthy project to sponsor for funding and Wally, never shy in any situation, piped up: "Have I got a project for you, Bill!" Conrad seconded his father's idea.

This time with both father and son acting as conduits between The North Face and the Clavey River Preservation Coalition, CRPC submitted its own Clavey River proposal to the Conservation Alliance. Glenda Edwards, a local Sierra Clubber who had become the cochair of the CRPC, says that Conrad was an enormous help, and "really held our hand through the whole process." Once complete, the proposal was fired off to Alliance board members, who came together at their next meeting to vote on the project. By then Conrad was following in his family's green footsteps and had asked TNF if he could represent it at

Conservation Alliance gatherings. It readily agreed, and Conrad took his new role seriously. When it was time to vote on the proposal, Conrad explained what the Clavey River meant—to him, to his family, to their community, and to the Greater Yosemite region. It was a moving and earnest speech that hit home with many of the industry representatives. Having read the proposal, the Alliance members were already impressed with its content—and with TRPT at its side, they were confident in the group's capabilities.

A Coalition with Megawatts

More than $20,000 was rushed off to help the group, whose annual operating budget was just over $11,000. Glenda, who had gotten involved in environmental issues years before, when she learned of the Forest Service's plan to dump massive herbicides on portions of the Stanislaus Forest, attributes much of the second phase of the CRPC's portion of the campaign to the second Conservation Alliance grant. "CRPC's efforts rose from the doldrums with the Alliance grant," she says. "We were able to send people to Washington [to lobby agencies for Wild and Scenic designation] and produce a beautiful color brochure and video for public outreach and fund-raising." Wally Anker agrees. "The support provided us a lot of leverage with other funders, and produced a certain level of intimidation among our opponents, too—to see a major industry supporting citizens like that."

They kicked off the second part of the campaign with the opening of the Water Shed, a funky yet inviting visitors information center that educated the public about the Tuolumne and Clavey Rivers. The converted shack was situated on a vacant lot in downtown Groveland—the space donated by the owner of the Iron Door Saloon across the street. Charles Little, who had been hired to run the center, was amazed at the response from visitors everywhere—especially the folks from San Francisco, who looked at photos of the Tuolumne and Hetch Hetchy, exclaiming, "So that's where our water comes from?" Ron Hunter also sent employees from the San

Francisco Patagonia store to help with the outreach as part of Patagonia's environmental internship program.

The other campaign strategy was more focused. Glenda Edwards and Johanna Thomas were working closely with Deputy Regional Forester Jean Hall. Jean was a compassionate woman of fifty-four who didn't agree with the "old school" of forestry—which managed the forest as a product for human consumption. She was an advocate for ecosystem protection and worked very hard to bring the agency around to a new way of thinking about the Clavey. Although Jean was in the last stages of a cancer that would take her life later that year, she continued to attend the meetings and support the group's position that the river deserved "suitability" status.

Conrad, upon returning from one of his international expeditions, did his own part by hosting a slide show of his adventures as a benefit for the coalition. "Conrad has a big following here in Tuolumne County," his father says proudly. "They've known him since he was a young boy, learning to rappel with the local Boy Scouts."

The People Are Heard

On July 25, 1996, the Forest Service released its anxiously awaited decision on the Clavey—this time recommending its suitability for Wild and Scenic status. It was an enormous leap toward permanent protection for the river—all that was needed now was for Congress to get its act together so a bill could be introduced. The *Clavey Cascade*, a newsletter put out jointly by CRPC and TRPT, hailed the decision and the contributions of Jean Hall, who had died in late October:

> *The Clavey River is honored to have gained a champion of such integrity and courage. Jean Hall stood up for her belief that the Forest Service has a responsibility to preserve important ecosystems, and she refused to cower before politi-*

cal pressure to make the easy, noncontroversial decisions. The
Forest Service has lost an extraordinary leader. In honor and
memory of Jean's life, those of us who love the Clavey pledge
to do everything within our ability to ensure that the Clavey
runs forever free.

Jean Hall must have thought highly of Tuolumne River Preservation Trust as well; she left the group a $5,000 bequest to be used specifically for lobbying Congress on a Wild and Scenic bill for the Clavey.

Conrad Anker's grandmother, who died in 1998, was able to see great steps taken toward permanent protection for the Clavey. She had the satisfaction of knowing that the Turlock Irrigation District had walked away from the Clavey and that forthcoming generations of Ankers would experience the Clavey as she had. The legacy of active, responsive citizenry that she had inspired in her son, and her son's son, was one of which she could be proud.

The Conservation Alliance was proud, too. With the Clavey's 47-mile stretch still free flowing, its corporate contributions had protected nearly 12,000 miles of river throughout the United States. Tipped vertically, that distance was taller than any mountain.

As for Conrad Anker, he looks forward to bringing his own clan back to Big Oak Flat and the banks of the Clavey River—where as a younger man he had walked with his father and scrambled on boulders. But first he's off to Antarctica to work on a film about global warming. "Who gives a rat's ass if you go and climb a mountain," he says, "when you can help your community save a river and really make a difference?"

BIBLIOGRAPHY

Clavey River Preservation Coalition, Tuolumne River Preservation Trust. *The Clavey Cascade* 1 (Summer 1993), 2 (Autumn 1994), 3 (Summer 1995), 4 (1996). San Francisco and Groveland, Calif.: Clavey River Preservation Coalition, Tuolumne River Preservation Trust, 1993–1996.

——. *Conserve the Clavey: the Central Sierra's Last Wild River.* Produced and directed by the Clavey River Preservation Coalition. 20 min. 3GP Productions, 1994. Videocassette.

——. *Grant Application to The Conservation Alliance.* Groveland, Calif.: Clavey River Preservation Coalition, 1994.

Houston Chronicle, 16 April 1996.

Modesto (Calif.) Bee, 22 August 1986–29 January 1995.

Muir, John. "Damming Hetch Hetchy." From unpublished journals, circa 1913. Available from Restore Hetch Hetchy, www.sierraclub.org/chapters/ca/hetchhetchy/damming.

——. *The Yosemite*. New York: The Century Company, 1912. Book scanned and converted to HTML, www.sc.org/john_muir-exhibit/writings/the_yosemite/index.html, by Dan Anderson, 1996.

The Tuolumne River Preservation Trust. *To Save the Clavey: A Proposal for Achieving Wild and Scenic Protection for California's Most Endangered River.* San Francisco: The Tuolumne River Preservation Trust, 1994.

Union Democrat (Sonora, Calif.), 20 July 1993–1 February 1995.

Restoration

Returning the Wolf to Maine's North Woods
1994–2000

> "If the land mechanism as a whole is good, then every part is good, whether we understand it or not. If the biota, in the course of aeons, has built something we . . . do not understand, then who but a fool would discard seemingly useless parts? To keep every cog and wheel is the first precaution of intelligent tinkering."
>
> —*Aldo Leopold*, Round River

Close your eyes. Envision yourself as one of your ancestors—an early settler encountering the New World. You are a real explorer, sans Gore-Tex, guidebooks, or Power Bars. You are surrounded by a primeval grove of ancient white pines, spruces draped with scarves of moss and thick clusters of ghostlike orchids. The place is so lush, so dense, that its darkness unnerves you. It is so vast that you can't imagine how to get out. Your family, which has followed you here in anticipation of a better life, is looking at you with wide, hopeful eyes. You are wet, cold, hungry. You need shelter and food.

You might not be able to see them, but you know they're here. Their sign is everywhere: Tracks and scat litter the mud. Branches crunch and snap as they slip through the shadows of the forest. You hear the cry of things not human. The call of a loon. Rutting elk. And then an aching, despairing howl. Spirit fingers tickle your neck and run the length of your spine.

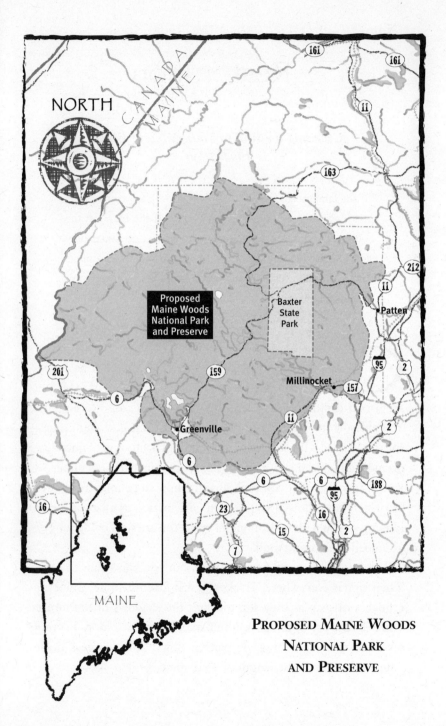

NORTH

CANADA
MAINE

161
161
11
163
212
11

Proposed
Maine Woods
National Park
and Preserve

Baxter
State
Park

Patten

201
95
2

6
159

Millinocket
157

11

Greenville

6

6
188
6

16
6
95

23
16

15
2

7

MAINE

**PROPOSED MAINE WOODS
NATIONAL PARK
AND PRESERVE**

You struggle for control, and subdue all that surrounds you—a visceral response to the fear this forest and its occupants have inspired. You could never replicate this scene, this mysterious cosmos of forest life—no matter what powers you had. But your needs, your family . . . there is no time to waste wondering, learning, about this place, its pieces. You will pass this fear on to your children, and they to theirs, until its origin is forgotten. Your bloodline will carry the fear of the unknown, the uncontrollable, forever in its bones.

A Modern Maine

Now fast-forward to the end of the twentieth century. You are standing in the same area with Michael Kellett, an environmentalist from Massachusetts. He has asked you to imagine what it was like to be one of those first European settlers, standing at the edge of the North Woods and peering in. You guess that it was overwhelming in size, terrifying in nature. He nods, knowing that these woods once spanned from the Atlantic Ocean to the Great Plains, and from Lake Superior to the Central Appalachian Highlands. He also knows what lived in these woods.

Formerly a regional director for The Wilderness Society, Kellett had a job that required time to learn about the pieces that once made New England whole—and then to try and put those pieces back together. He has continued to study the puzzle long enough now to know that the key parts lie here. In northern Maine, he believes, is America's greatest remnant of the North Woods.

But Michael Kellett is under the gun. The clock is ticking to restore this wilderness—a place Henry David Thoreau described in 1846 as "primeval, untamed, and forever untameable." That was before the new landowners, the paper corporations, got their hands on this once-vast ecosystem.

It's not so vast anymore. But it is terrifying—only not in the way you imagine. In just one generation, Kellett says, an area larger than the state of Delaware has been clear-cut. The land has been fractured by thousands of logging roads. The countless lakes and streams seem lifeless—dams and the warm, silted waters have blocked the spawning of the Atlantic salmon. Kellett explains that this delicious fish, on which your ancestors feasted, is nearly gone—with a population of only two or three thousand remaining in all New England. The Canada lynx, American marten, and spruce grouse, formerly abundant, are now infrequent. In fact, as the North Woods have dwindled, nearly 25 percent of Maine's native plants and nonmarine animals have become endangered, threatened, rare, or extinct.

That's why the wolf is gone, and why Michael Kellett must act swiftly.

Our War with the Wolf

What Kellett doesn't understand is why so much fear and hatred of this species lingers. Wolves have never lived up to the man-eating myth they inspired. There has never been a single documented case of a healthy wolf killing a human, and the great canines turned to livestock only after we wiped out all their natural prey. Even now, as we step into the twenty-first century, in areas where the wolf and its normal diet of wild ungulates have been successfully restored to their ecosystems, wolves are responsible for only a fraction of 1 percent of livestock killings. And when they do bring down a domestic animal, funds are quickly raised and made readily available by Defenders of Wildlife, a national environmental organization, to compensate the rancher at fair market value.

The hysteria began long ago—the meat of fairy tales and horror stories. Beginning in the 1600s, before we understood how wolves act as sentries for the wild world, the American colonies posted bounties on the animals, fearing they would otherwise prey on humans and compete with them for food—like deer, moose, and beaver. Wolf killings were cruel and extensive—and took place with the same rabidity as the Salem witch trials.

Northeastern lore recalls that one village tried to kill the last pack in the region by driving them to the top of a mountain and setting its summit on fire. The great predators went up in flames while the villagers cheered. The few remaining eastern timber wolves (a subspecies of the gray wolf) retreated to Canada.

According to Kellett, people didn't realize that without the wolf, the North Woods would begin to fall to pieces, like a jigsaw puzzle pushed off a kitchen table. The numbers of other animal populations went askew. Some have argued that what humans kill makes up for the wolves—and therefore the balance of things is kept in check. But Rick Bass, in his best-seller *The Ninemile Wolves*, points out that, in hunting for prey, wolves "halt at the edge of the so-critical gap, that invisible line where hunger crosses over into greed." In this sense wolves differ from us: When the large canids roamed the North Woods, they supplied a sense of balance and proportion to the region's delicately pieced-together functions of life—while humans have managed to tip the North Woods' evolutionary scale on its face.

One Man's Impatience

Kellett recognizes how we have done this. In the blink of an evolutionary eye, nearly the entire region was tamed into its current quaint pastoral scenes of farms and towns. Even our thirst for blood sports hasn't kept deer and moose from overpopulating. And the forest suffers because of the amount of forage the bloated populations consume. But parts of northern Maine are different, Kellett says. There you can still see the wild, wondrous remains of the wilderness that made our ancestors shake in their boots.

Years ago Kellett worked for a large national group, but he felt buried beneath a mountain of bureaucracy and muzzled by the organization's aversion to controversy. It gnawed at him; he had ideas about how to restore the North Woods and all of its vital parts. He ran the ideas past his colleagues in the conservation community, but their response was demoralizing. "They all said it was politically infeasible, and that the situation up there wasn't all that bad," he says. "They actually told me that the timber companies were doing a pretty good job and that I should just go back to Massachusetts and work on something else."

Even the recognizable fragments of the great North Woods in northern Maine are scattered, surrounded by bare dirt and amputated tree stumps. In some places newly planted monocrops of scraggly trees grow in neat uniform rows. In just one hundred years, much of Maine had been bought up by less than two dozen transnational corporations and private trusts—the largest concentration of industrial ownership and the highest proportion of foreign land ownership of anywhere in the United States. Much of the legendary ancient forest had been reduced to a "working forest," dedicated to commercial harvest of timber and paper fiber.

"This is the New England we have come to know," Kellett says. "We've forgotten the old New England, which the North Woods covered. Now imagining big wilderness in the East is totally counterintuitive."

Kellett, born into the urban jungle of Detroit, Michigan, where every inch of lakefront was surrounded by homes, where every stretch of land was plowed down in the name of growth, will never forget the precious moments he has found in wild places. Places like the North Woods.

But people need jobs, you argue. Your father and his father before him always told you that the forest provides jobs for people. What they didn't know was that by 1999, tourism in Maine would generate more jobs than fishing, forestry, and farming combined. Kellett points out that the environmentalists haven't taken away the woods jobs; rather, the timber companies themselves—through globalization, mechanization, and poor forest stewardship—eliminated 40 percent of woods jobs and almost 20 percent of mill positions. In 1960 one out of every eleven Mainers worked for the timber industry, but by 1996 that number was less than one in twenty-three.

He asks if you have listened to the howl of a real wolf in the wild. You have to admit, you have heard little save the hollow, metallic growl of industry.

But Kellett has a vision. His mind's eye has pulled into sharp focus the restoration of a wilderness big enough for wolves. He feels a sort of kinship with the wolf. He relates to its pack mentality—its need for community and social order, its fierce defense of territory, its loyalty to a mate and family. He sees how the wolf uses the strength of numbers to defeat the most daunting of prey, like a moose or a bear. He also understands its need for space and freedom and wildness. He understands that in captivity, the spirit of the wolf withers. He understands that when the wolf goes, so do all things wild.

RESTORE Is Born

In 1987 Kellett finally resigned from his big national job to become a sort of lone wolf. With his nose to the ground, he began searching for his own territory, in the hope of recruiting a small and aggressive pack to join him. He connected with Dave Carle, a young environmentalist from the Appalachian Mountain Club, and in 1992 they founded RESTORE: The North Woods. Some of their goals included seeking protection for northern Maine's endangered animals and their habitat, halting destructive logging practices, and rehabilitating watersheds. But one of their priorities was to call home the long-lost *Canis lupus*, the gray wolf of the Northeast. The animal was the stick with which they would measure the restoration of the North Woods.

By 1994 RESTORE was well on its way, having convinced the federal government to propose listing the Atlantic salmon as threatened on a number of Maine's rivers. They also slowed some of the clear-cutting, and collected thousands of signatures on a petition calling for reintroduction of the wolf. All this came out of Michael Kellett's home in Concord, Massachusetts, which served as RESTORE's first office. Space was tight; the fax machine was housed in the spare bedroom.

Moose are just one species dependent upon Maine's North Woods.

It was a start, but Michael Kellett and Dave Carle were thinking *big*.

They honed a Maine Woods Reserve proposal that Kellett had designed during his days at The Wilderness Society; later that same year they announced a plan to protect 3.2 million acres of the Maine Woods—an area the size of Yellowstone and Yosemite Parks combined—as a joint national park and preserve. Although their goal was wildness, not a theme park with traffic jams and espresso stands, the two men figured the region had enough human contact to prevent its immediately qualifying for congressional wilderness designation—which requires that "the impacts of man be substantially unnoticeable." Instead, the proposal described a "restoration park," similar to Great Smoky Mountains, Redwood, Shenandoah, and Voyageurs. The park and preserve would acquire private land from willing sellers, parcel by parcel. Logging and other industrial uses would, over time, be phased out. Permanently out of the hands of developers and timber tycoons, the area's wild character would be rejuvenated. The park and preserve would be the linchpins for RESTORE's broader vision: to reestablish major portions of the North Woods across the northeastern states and Canada. The ultimate goal was, and is, big, true wilderness—the kind found only in Alaska.

Public Vs. Private Land Protection

Michael Kellett knows there can't be true wilderness without the wolf, and that a wolf isn't a wolf without true wilderness. He thinks that turning the private lands into public ones is the answer. A man who has spent much time exploring the West and its wide expanses of federally managed land, he loves and understands the concept of public lands—held in trust by government agencies for the people. The people have a say in how these lands are managed, and there is a process by which to do so. To him, the statistic that less than 4 percent of Maine is publicly owned translates to mean that the public has little influence over the fate of their state's natural heritage.

"What if Maine had more public land?" Kellett asked. Many scratched their heads. They had thought there was enough land, enough resources, for everybody to get what they needed. And the mantra of private property rights was part of the cultural legacy. But time with Kellett taught many Maine residents that wolves really are just wolves and nothing else; that we are their greatest threat, not the other way around. Residents learned how recent fish and game policies boosted once-depleted populations of moose, deer, and beavers, setting the stage for the wolves to return. And they have witnessed how private landowners have damaged the land.

Others have had Michael Kellett's vision to protect the Maine Woods. Thoreau wrote an entire book titled *The Maine Woods*, and after his 1853 visit, he advocated that such places become "national preserves." Over the next few decades, many proposals for Maine Woods protection were put forth. In 1919 state representative Percival P. Baxter pushed for state protection that would have encompassed lands surrounding Mount Katahdin, the highest peak in the area and terminus for the Appalachian Trail, saying, "The works of men are short-lived. Monuments decay, buildings crumble, wealth vanishes, but Katahdin and its massive grandeur will forever remain the mountain of the people of Maine." When the proposal was defeated, the future governor of Maine purchased more than 200,000 acres of the region with his own money, turning it over to the state to be managed as "forever wild" Baxter State Park.

The Park Plan

RESTORE reminds us that this is the heart of Thoreau country, a quintessential American landscape from which our nation's character and heritage developed. The region nurses the headwaters of five major rivers and nearly 110 miles of the Appalachian Trail—including the famed "100-Mile Wilderness." The proposed park would serve as a mecca for skiing, hiking, canoeing, and fishing, while the surrounding preserve would still allow hunting and even snowmobiling—all escapes from the rest of New England's domestic banality. There are innumerable cultural treasures too: Revolutionary War routes and Native American sites dot these forests. Who better than the National Park Service, guardian of Mesa Verde and Gettysburg, to protect such history?

In its park proposal RESTORE addressed the economics of park protection versus current private ownership. The timber and paper companies had devastated many of the local economies with their downsizing, while studies demonstrated that a park/preserve would stimulate local economies by creating new jobs and businesses. RESTORE's figures indicate that the state's economy would see a boost of between $109 and $435 million in annual retail sales, and support 5,000 to 20,000 jobs. What's more, the park boundaries would only encompass one-fifth of the state's commercial forestland; four-fifths would remain open to sustainable forestry practices—part of the bigger picture RESTORE would tackle later on. The clever spin RESTORE used to announce the billion-dollar pricetag for the nation's second largest park is, "It would cost less than one B-2 Stealth bomber."

Still, many criticized RESTORE's plan, insisting that conservation easements were the way to go. Some held that national parks get "loved to death." Kellett counters, "When I hear all the happy talk about public-private partnerships, I just say, 'Yeah, right.' I have yet to see it work. By my estimation, North Maine is a disaster, precisely because it is privately owned. Even the worst National Forest is managed better than those private properties up there . . . a big national park—with connecting reserve lands surrounding it—would be the best solution for true ecosystem protection."

The Pack Grows but the Trees Fall

By 1995 the group had a membership of 650 aggressive citizens, nipping at the heels of decision makers and agencies to consider a national park designation. The growing pack of maverick greens opened an office in Maine and hired Maine native Jym St. Pierre to run it. They also hired a young woman named Kristin DeBoer, fresh out of Antioch with a master's in environmental sciences. Kellett was so impressed with her fearlessness and her aversion to "so-called political realities," that eventually he handed her the wolf program. It was a time to establish credibility, for both wolf reintroduction as well as the park proposal, and DeBoer, articulate, intelligent, and well read, had no trouble rising to the occasion.

But RESTORE needed more publicity, and it needed even more activists to pressure the government. And things were getting worse for the forest. FOR SALE signs were sprouting like mushrooms throughout the Maine Woods. In response to business setbacks, the timber and paper companies were dumping their Maine Woods real estate at a breathtaking rate; sometimes investors bought up the $200-per-acre timberland on lakeshores only to turn around and sell it to developers for $70,000 per acre. By the mid-1990s permits for more than 5,000 houses or camps would be granted, and 200,000 acres would be subdivided. It was a bit of a scam; many buyers cracked open their nest eggs for a wilderness dream home and signed on the dotted line before they noticed that a thin veil of trees, not a forest, was all the companies left alongside their lots. In *Sierra*, Ted Williams wrote of flying over these areas with Rudy Engholm, a volunteer pilot for Northern Wings, which, as Williams put it, "shows reporters, politicians, and resource managers the difference between what industry press releases say the earth looks like and what it really looks like." Engholm had once been a software executive in Ann Arbor, Michigan, but when developers felled an enormous oak tree behind his house, he packed up and hightailed it to Maine. There he joined RESTORE. Flying with Engholm, Williams was appalled at the land behind what he calls the "beauty strip," saying that it's "not just in bad shape, it's *gone.*" Rudy Engholm agreed. "I burn wood," he told Williams. "I'm not against cutting trees. But I believe there's a difference between a haircut and a scalping."

Ravenous for Resources

Money was tight; many foundations had rejected RESTORE's requests for funding because they couldn't see big wilderness in the East, and because they didn't have faith that the northeastern wolf could be more than a political animal. It was a nerve-racking time, and without a bigger bank account, the effort risked losing energy.

One day Michael received a call from Walter Bickford, a former Massachusetts Fish and Wildlife Commissioner he'd known during the Dukakis era in Massachusetts. A down-to-earth sportsman who spent his time hunting and fishing in the woods of northern Maine, Bickford had since been hired as the environmental administrator at Malden Mills, a manufacturing company famous for its recycled fleece fabric—spun from used soda-pop bottles.

Bickford was representing Malden in the Outdoor Industry Conservation Alliance (OICA) and had followed RESTORE's efforts. He thought the group was a great candidate for a grant. Kellett was thrilled—especially because he knew what a passionate hunter and angler Bickford was. The fact that Bickford understood how wilderness and parks and wolves fit together, that he grasped how it would protect his outdoor experience in the long run, was impressive. "He's way ahead of the curve," Michael says.

Bickford and a handful of other outdoor industry representatives in the Alliance promoted the hell out of RESTORE at the next OICA meeting. With his support the Conservation Alliance took the plunge, committing $35,000 to the group. "People can paint the Conservation Alliance and these other outdoor companies as middle-of-the-road corporate folks who get off easy by just giving money," says Michael Kellett. "But they had vision and took a gamble with us."

With the infusion of funds, RESTORE's campaigns pounced into the national spotlight, galvanizing public support for both a national park feasibility study and a wolf reintroduction program. Other outdoor industry leaders, like REI and Patagonia, also provided crucial financial support at a time when many continued to question the "political feasibility" of RESTORE's efforts. Thanks to the Conservation Alliance, the campaign was howling. Activist workshops were conducted, and thousands more park proposal brochures were printed and distributed. Newspapers and magazines across the nation began talking about a Maine Woods National Park. The national and regional environmental groups that had once scoffed at Kellett's idea were beginning to come on board, touting the park as one of their priorities. And when the public began to see how a rash of so-called conservation easements could still allow for logging and other industrial activities, RESTORE's park proposal gained some muscle. Suddenly RESTORE's vision was capturing the public's imagination.

The Sporting Fallacy

The next thing RESTORE knew, the *Maine Times* ran an editorial titled "The Welcome Mat Ought to Be Out for Wolves." It lambasted hunters, calling their bias against wolves "irrational and selfish." The editorial pointed to the unwise irony that the Department of Inland Fisheries and Wildlife, which manages Maine's wild creatures, is funded by hunting and fishing license fees—questioning the agency's ability to make effective decisions on behalf of the wolf. "Sooner or later we are going to learn that shooting animals is not the only or best way to enjoy the outdoors— or even attract new jobs to the hinterlands," the paper wrote.

"Already, the value of the moose to tourism significantly exceeds revenue from the moose hunt." Another local editorial followed and dismantled hunters' arguments that the wolves would kill off everything by stating unequivocally, "Wolves and their prey evolved in nature together. Were wolves going to exterminate their prey, they would have done so long before man nearly exterminated the wolf."

With the surge in momentum came a backlash from private property rights activists, the timber companies, and wise-use groups. *Sports Afield* writer Monte Burke wrote that Maine may have "the smallest percentage of public lands in the nation, but [it also has] the greatest amount of public access to private lands." He added that this "right" was a "politically cemented tradition that dates to colonial times (1647) when King Charles I decreed that all private land could be 'fished and fowled.'" In northern Maine this meant that hunters and anglers had carte blanche access to corporate-owned lands. It was worth it for the timber giants—along with the wise-use groups that they funded—to keep the sportspeople on their side. If they didn't, as Ted Williams pointed out in *Orion* magazine, sportspeople and environmentalists—at least 65 percent of the population—would unite into what he called "an absolutely irresistible coalition." Wise-use groups like the Blue Ribbon Coalition and the Maine Conservation Rights Institute thus targeted their property rights arguments at hunters and anglers—who listened. George Smith, for instance, the executive director of the Sportsmen's Alliance of Maine, called RESTORE "a very radical organization seeking to lock up our state and make it a playground for out-of-staters." He failed to address the counterarguments that visiting national parks is one of America's favorite pastimes—and that next to wilderness designation, only the intensive, broad-based protection a park offers would ensure healthy fish and game populations. The park would continue to allow fishing, while the preserve lands around it would still provide hunting opportunities.

Besides, the sportspeople were not responding to the logging land-lords' real estate blitz—which meant that their access was becoming all the more precarious. Still, the hunters and anglers took to Smith's arguments hook, line, and sinker.

Brock Evans, a noted wilderness and forest activist who helped pass countless wilderness bills in his time, sat on the RESTORE board. A former vice president of the National Audubon Society, Evans was cheering for RESTORE's goals 100 percent. He dismissed the opposition and the cynics, writing that "through all national parks campaigns over the past century, there are two common threads: intense and ferocious opposition from the 'wise use' people, special interests, and naysayers; and second, the courage and steady perseverance of ordinary folks who loved their land and were determined to rescue it. . . . They just went on and did it anyway. . . . Our own history tells us that there is absolutely no reason why people cannot accomplish the exact same thing in the great Maine Woods." His words were comforting and inspiring to the small band of forest defenders. He kept the momentum going when opposition was hitting from all sides.

A Political Animal

Meanwhile, the wolf was gaining ground—thanks to the efforts of Kristin DeBoer and others. DeBoer, in addition to her RESTORE duties, coordinated CREW—the Coalition to Restore the Eastern Wolf. Where RESTORE had once been a solitary interloper among the federal and state agencies, there were at this point thirty organizations working collaboratively on wolf restoration in Maine and other parts of New England. "The idea is to synthesize wilderness and wolf recovery," DeBoer says. "We don't want to bring back wolves just to have them roaming through clear-cuts as if they were open-air zoos. We want the whole ecosystem put back together."

By 1999 CREW was cranking. They held a northeastern wolf conference—the first of its kind—and saw a slew of good press afterward. Their efforts were bolstered by a study that claimed that intact forested lands from upstate New York to Maine could hold approximately 1,300 wolves. As proof of the growing favor of the public, an opinion poll demonstrated that an overwhelming 79 percent of Mainers supported some level of wolf recovery in their state.

Meanwhile, the wolf was having trouble in other parts of the country—Secretary of the Interior Bruce Babbitt proposed delisting the animal as a concession to ranchers and timber interests, which worried that the Endangered Species Act would restrict their activities if wolves roamed the land. A New Hampshire state representative publicly aired his concerns for hikers and tourists, saying that he "didn't think it would be appreciated . . . if there could be a pack of wolves attacking them at night." Meanwhile, New Hampshire protesters wore prison stripes and carried signs that read: WOLVES WOULD MAKE US PRISONERS IN OUR HOMES as their legislature passed a bill that barred wolf recovery within state boundaries.

But in Maine the pack of greens brought down its prey. Thanks largely to media attention and the 200,000 citizen signatures CREW collected, the U.S. Fish and Wildlife Service finally consented to consider an eastern recovery plan for the gray wolf. Science supports such a plan, too: Paul Nickerson, who heads the Massachusetts regional endangered species office for the U.S. Fish and Wildlife Service, now oversees the program. "The only thing this food chain lacks is a top predator," he told *Northern Woodlands*. "Speaking just as a biologist, I think to make this a complete food chain, the wolf has a place in it."

Approaching Wholeness

RESTORE continues to gain support for the park and preserve as well. With increased outreach efforts, it has signed on 300 businesses as park proponents. Many of these are outdoor recreation companies that are also members of the Conservation Alliance, but others include mom-and-pop concerns that have suffered through the timber industry's abandonment of many northern Maine towns. Gifted nature writers like Terry Tempest Williams join arms with political representatives and scientists from across the nation to support the establishment of a Maine Woods National Park. Celebrities are signing on, too; Christopher Reeve became a new kind of superhero by flying in an airplane over the proposed park and committing his "wholehearted support to this bold, timely effort." And in May 2000 *Down East* magazine stated that "a park of some sort [in the Maine Woods] is likely to be the major conservation issue of the next decade."

Every other form of land use or protection effort is beginning to be compared to the national park idea. By July 2000 a Sierra Club public opinion poll showed that 63 percent of Mainers favored a three-million-acre park—and the poll results were printed on the front page of Maine's most conservative paper. Activists everywhere are now promoting the park in their own ways. Beth Wheatley, the Maine Woods coordinator for RESTORE, took it upon herself to "Pedal for the Park," a strenuous effort in which she rode 500 miles from the Adirondacks in New York to the Maine Woods, giving presentations in towns along the way. The activist group Forest Ecology Network has joined forces with RESTORE to have a little fun with the park idea, placing official-looking signs informing tourists they are heading toward Maine Woods National Park in the front yards of supporters who live in the proposed park's gateway communities. The campaign is characterized as a playful twist on the old Maine saying, "You can't get there from here."

But apparently the wolves can get there from Canada. It is as if they sniffed the wind and found that Maine was giving off a more welcoming air. In the last seven years, two individual wolves have been sighted in the Maine Woods—though unfortunately they were shot and killed by hunters. And another was apparently spotted by hunter Dana Smith, who said, "I got thirty-some years in the woods . . . this wasn't no coyote." Smith had the grace and wisdom to take his finger off the trigger as the wolf loped away.

The lesson in these wolf sightings? The wilderness of New England is already returning to wholeness. This physical evolution is becoming a political reality, too, by the citizens and companies supporting the establishment of a national park and preserve.

Beth Wheatley prepares to begin her 500-mile "Pedal for the Park."

Michael Kellett is pleased how his pack has grown; its instinct for defending Maine's wolves and wilderness is sharper than ever. He looks north toward Canada, as if hoping to spot another wayward wolf heading south, in search of new territory, and smiles. "We could really begin the twenty-first century with a howl in the Northeast."

Returning to this forest in the ancestor's body, you see the North Woods differently now; not a palette of dark shadows but a puzzle of vibrant, complex pieces that fit together in ways you are learning to understand. Some of it you will never comprehend, but when the wolf bays this time your pulse pounds with delight, not terror. You know now that the wolf is your brother and that if you are frugal, you can each feed your family from these same woods. The wolf's presence is a sign that you haven't meddled too much; that these great woods—these keepers of the oldest trees, the clearest streams, the hardiest salmon and moose—will also keep our spirits and our heritage from withering.

BIBLIOGRAPHY

Bass, Rick. *The Ninemile Wolves.* New York: Clark City Press, 1992.

Burke, Monte. "The Yellowstone of the East?" *Sports Afield,* March 2000, 13–16.

Busch, Robert M. *The Wolf Almanac.* 2nd ed. New York: The Lyons Press, 1995.

Cole, John. "For Sale: Maine." *Country Journal,* March/April 2000, 46–50.

Conuel, Thomas. "Bring It All Back." *Sanctuary: The Journal of the Massachusetts Audubon Society* 36, no. 3 (1997): 6–9.

Dillon, John. "The Gray Wolf Is Howling at the Northeast's Door." *Northern Woodlands,* Autumn 1999, 27–30.

Evans, Brock. "National Parks?—Piece of Cake!" *North Woods Vision* 4, no. 1 (1996): 4.

Harden, Blaine. "Who Best to Protect the North Woods?" *Washington Post,* 24 August 1998, A1–A6, col. 3.

Kellett, Michael J. "Maine Woods National Park: The Best Way to Restore the Wild." *Wild Earth* 10, no. 2 (2000): 60–64.

———. "Why a Maine Woods National Park?" *North Woods Vision* 4, no. 1 (1996): 2.

Leopold, Aldo. *Round River.* New York: Oxford University Press, 1993.

"Maine Park Advocates Shoot for 100,000 Signatures." *Maine Times,* 2 September 1999, 6.

"N.H. Timber Workers Say No to Plan for Wolves." *Portland (Maine) Press Herald*, 1 October 1998.

RESTORE: The North Woods. *Maine Woods National Park: Saving the Heart of Maine.* Concord, Mass.: RESTORE: The North Woods, 1995.

St. Pierre, Jym. "A Wildland Under Siege." *North Woods Vision* 4, no. 1 (1996): 3.

"A 3-Million Acre National Park in Maine? You Bet." *Mainebiz*, June 1999, 16–19.

"Welcome Mat Ought to Be Out for the Wolves." *Maine Times*, 3 April 1997, 10.

Williams, Ted. "Thoreau's Dream." *Sierra*, March/April 1999, 58–65.

———. "The Cost of Division: Is the Wise-Use Movement Sabotaging an Alliance Between Sportsmen and Environmentalists?" *Orion*, Summer 2000, 48–54.

It Takes a Village

Headwaters Forest, California
1985–1999

The timber wars over Headwaters Forest had splintered entire towns. For days radicals hung in the treetops like a family of primates, their banners pleading SAVE THE OLD GROWTH! Loggers stood below, stabbing the air with middle fingers, hurling black words at the tree sitters. Other folks stood helplessly on the edge of the forest, looking in, blocked by local law enforcement as the chain saws roared and the great red trees thundered to the ground.

It was as if the roots of the trees had spread out into the world, entangling humans in their fate. They had snagged the attention of many, including a young college student named Doug Riley-Thron. In Arcata he had seen the ancient trees; every hour they passed by the Volvo lot where he washed cars after classes. The redwoods were bound by chains to the backs of semis—trees so large that only one or two could fit on each truck bed. But it was a bit like seeing prepackaged meat in the supermarket: You didn't think too much about how it came to be that way—a living creature killed, its body cut up and prepared to sell for human consumption.

Now Riley-Thron wanted to see the trees of Headwaters—upright, roots and limbs attached, alive. After getting directions, the twenty-one-year-old drove as far as he could before stashing his car and trespassing over Pacific Lumber's property line.

There were thousands of acres of trees before him, but plenty of hiking remained before Riley-Thron would see the two-thousand-

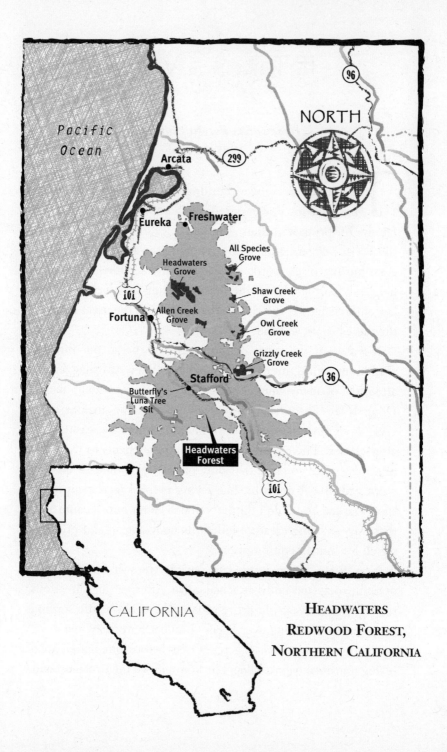

Pacific
Ocean

NORTH

Arcata

Eureka

Freshwater

All Species
Grove

Headwaters
Grove

Shaw Creek
Grove

Allen Creek
Grove

Owl Creek
Grove

Fortuna

Grizzly Creek
Grove

Stafford

Butterfly's
Luna Tree
Sit

Headwaters
Forest

CALIFORNIA

HEADWATERS
REDWOOD FOREST,
NORTHERN CALIFORNIA

year-old ones. His map indicated that the last of the ancient red-woods were scattered into six groves. As he hiked he saw that the old groves were laced together by silt-laden creeks and miles of clear-cuts, some still smoldering from the company's postlogging slash and burns. It looked like a war zone.

After several hours Riley-Thron reached the edge of the primeval forest. He entered, thankful to hear no shouts or saws nearby. He stood motionless, then slowly turned in a circle.

Every metaphor had been used by others before him: Cathedrals. Gentle giants. But for the young man who had left Texas when his last hiking spot had been swallowed by the George Bush Highway, there were no words. There were only immense beings—and a thrum of life both singular and plural. It was like entering a closely knit village.

Their strength is in their numbers. A tangle of intertwined roots, only in solidarity can they deflect wind and rain. They share a communal rooftop, a communal foundation, and the poetry of species in between: bay laurel, spotted owl, leopard lily, truffle-eating red tree vole.

None survive alone. It is a clan effort, sustained and guided by the ancients.

Standing among the trees, Riley-Thron cocked his ear and listened to their pulse. Then he vowed his life to saving this collective of beings. It was 1992.

A Company Gone Astray

At the time Pacific Lumber (PL) wasn't taking just the grande dames—trees often twenty feet in diameter that predated Christ's birth. The company was also slicing and dicing everything on the slope, then lathering the raw, exposed soil with a thick coat of herbicides to kill undergrowth that would compete with its replants. Even the steepest hillsides, held in place only by the tree roots, were being clear-cut. When the rains came, the poisoned soil would wash away, gathering stumps and boulders as it descended.

Midslope, it became a twenty-foot wall of mud, gaining speed. Down it went, eventually coming to rest in the streambeds. It poisoned and warmed the water, which became undrinkable for humans and uninhabitable for salmon.

Whatever Pacific Lumber said in defense of its practices, the facts were stacked against it. The truth was, when the trees went down, an entire community of life went with them. The marbled murrelet, an enigmatic little shorebird whose numbers were in rapid decline, relied on the ancient treetops in Headwaters as one of only three coastal nesting areas in California. California's coho salmon was also threatened with extinction. Ten percent of the remaining population depended upon the Headwaters streams and rivers for spawning, but the fish were unable to survive in the warm, oxygen-deprived waters downhill from PL's logging operations.

The timber industry often defended clear-cutting with the justification that animals would adapt to second- or third-growth forests. But a tree farm can't replace the ancient ecosystem, and such a complex, inextricably interdependent community of living creatures and microclimates would take centuries to re-create—if ever they could be re-created.

When corporations argued that animals could look for other forests, environmentalists countered that it was hard to imagine the rare southern torrent salamander—a creature entirely dependent upon ancient downed logs, with their fungi and moisture—making a run for it across miles of slash and stumps, in the glare of the hot sun, looking for another cool, wet, ancient forest to call home. And spotted owls are reluctant to cross an opening even the size of a football field, because they are so vulnerable to larger winged predators like the great horned owl. Instead the juvenile owls opt to starve to death at the edge of clear-cuts.

Indeed, there was nowhere for the salamander to run or the owls to seek cover. More than 96 percent of the ancient forest was gone, a forest that only 200 years ago had draped much of California's and Oregon's coastal hills.

Under the auspices of the Murphy family, which founded the business in 1869, Pacific Lumber had been a different kind of company. Generations of Humboldt County residents had worked there, and had been well provided for. The company's conservative cutting practices ensured that it had old trees and healthy forests long after other lumber companies had cut all of theirs down. PL never used herbicides, never cut on steep slopes, and protected the watersheds.

The Hex of Hurwitz

And PL's practices had left it rich with assets—living assets. It owned the largest remaining privately held stand of old-growth redwoods in the world. Because of the trees and their potential to produce rapid cash flow, PL caught the eye of Charles Hurwitz, a corporate raider from Texas. In 1986, in a sly and hostile takeover, Hurwitz's Maxxam Corporation gobbled up the company—using an infamous junk bond king and a $900 million deal with more than $700 million in high-interest, high-risk debt. The tight-lipped Texan, a man who rarely granted interviews and was hardly seen outside his small social circle, was eventually sued by the Office of Thrift Supervision and the Federal Deposit Insurance Corporation for illegally manipulating assets held by the United Savings Association of Texas—of which Hurwitz was the dominating shareholder. The agencies alleged that this manipulation was intended to help fund the PL takeover—and that it caused the savings and loan to fail. The result was a $1.6 billion taxpayer-funded bailout; to date it is the third largest savings-and-loan scandal in U.S. history.

Shortly after the PL takeover, Hurwitz flew to the company's headquarters in Scotia, California, where he announced to his employees his version of the Golden Rule: "He who has the gold, rules." Hurwitz then ordered the loggers to liquidate the old growth—of which PL owned more than all other timber companies in the world combined—by tripling, and in some cases quadrupling, its rate of logging. He didn't seem to care that the very last of the old redwoods—save the few token stands in national and state parks—would be gone in a few years. Hurwitz also milked $60 million from PL's employee pension fund. Both schemes were designed to generate fast cash for repaying the massive debt assumed when he acquired the company.

Pacific Lumber's employees were stunned. The company they knew had vaporized overnight. Still, PL was the largest employer in the county, and few other jobs were available. Most had no choice but to put up and shut up.

The Violence Begins

But thanks to the efforts of three local Earth First! activists, who comprised the self-proclaimed Redwood Action Team (RAT), people like Doug Riley-Thron were beginning to learn about Headwaters and the fight to stop the savage logging practices of Charles Hurwitz. One RAT leader, Greg King, had spent days suspended high in the trees targeted for cutting, trying to keep the chain saws at bay. Darryl Cherney beckoned the media to cover King's dramatic protests. Judi Bari organized the supporters—grandmothers, ranchers, hippies, even loggers. She had hundreds of them swarming the lumber mills, chaining themselves to bulldozers, and rallying in the streets of PL's towns.

RAT's direct actions focused the public's attention on Headwaters, and this infuriated PL bosses and supervisors. A smear campaign was organized, accusing RAT of tree spiking and other violent acts. Although RAT had a strict code against any form of violence, and although its message to the loggers was, "Your jobs will be gone when the trees are gone," nearly the entire logging community turned on them. One logger said it was easier to punch a tree hugger than to fight an amorphous, all-powerful corporate entity.

Death threats began to haunt RAT's leading trio, and local law enforcement officers refused to investigate. In 1989 Bari's car was rammed from behind by a logging truck at full speed; Bari's two children were sitting in the backseat at the time. Fortunately, no one was hurt. Mendocino County supervisor Marilyn Butcher said only, "You brought it on yourself, Judi."

But in May of the following year, Bari and Cherney were in the Bay Area organizing for Redwood Summer, their biggest event yet, when a bomb—handmade from eleven inches of galvanized pipe, gunpowder, and a sheath of nails—exploded beneath the driver's seat in Bari's car. The seat blew into pieces that embedded in Judi's backside, shattering her tailbone and permanently crippling her right leg. Shrapnel marred Cherney's face, and his eardrums ruptured. Before Bari was even out of surgery, the FBI and Oakland Police Department placed her, along with Cherney, under arrest. They announced to the press that the two activists were "terrorists" and the only suspects in the bombing. Other suspects, although numerous, were never investigated. Despite the incident and at Bari's insistence, Redwood Summer went on without her.

Laying Down the Law

Earth First!'s Redwood Action Team wasn't the only group fighting for Headwaters. By 1991 the Environmental Protection Information Center (EPIC), a tiny local group based in Garberville, California, had on behalf of angry citizens filed lawsuits challenging Pacific Lumber's harvest plans in the Headwaters groves. Many of the suits had slowed or halted several of the company's harvest plans. On March 12, 1992, the marbled murrelet was listed as a California endangered species, an event that would give EPIC the legal upper hand. But the very next day, the California Board of Forestry approved a plan to log Owl Creek, even though the California Department of Forestry (CDF) had flatly rejected it. EPIC and the Sierra Club sued, charging that PL's harvest plan would violate the Endangered Species Act. The groups convinced the judge to require the board to reconsider its plan and order a murrelet survey. PL conducted the survey hastily and mailed it off to the agencies.

But before the spit on the envelope's seal was dry, PL began a surprise assault on Owl Creek's old growth. On a Sunday—Father's Day—PL ordered its loggers in to work with the command to drop as many trees as possible. After three days PL had become a million dollars richer off illegally cut old growth. The feds finally intervened, beginning negotiations with PL that lasted through the summer and fall. When talks broke for the Thanksgiving weekend, the agencies made it clear to PL officials that they had in no way received permission yet to harvest more old growth.

But the day after Thanksgiving, a local biologist named Chuck Powell entered Owl Creek Grove with the intent of viewing the Father's Day carnage. Instead he was witness to a new crime: In thirty minutes he heard eight ancient trees fall as the loggers rushed to topple the forest.

Powell drove like hell back to town to contact EPIC and the feds. EPIC was outraged; the agencies, apathetic. EPIC's attorney, Mark Harris, was told by one official, "Is this *really* such a big deal, Mark? It's only some trees." When Harris successfully sought an emergency stay, which finally stopped the illegal harvesting, PL complained that the downed wood would rot, just lying there in the forest. Although there was ample evidence that old-growth redwood takes ages to rot—the reason its "Clear Heart" wood is so valuable in the first place—the court allowed the company to remove another million dollars' worth of illegal logs from the grove.

Again EPIC charged into court, denouncing PL's harvest plan. Mark Harris was a young surfer new to the world of law, but he was focused and furious. For days he worked in the bungalow that EPIC used as an office, sleeping on the floor for only brief moments and eating only when staff members brought him food. Up against San Francisco's most notorious prodevelopment law firms, Harris knew his argument had to be flawless. As luck would have it, Colorado attorney Macon Cowles had caught wind of PL's doings at about this time and blew a fuse. A diehard environmental advocate, Cowles rushed to Harris's aid. Together the two found that PL had obscured seventy detections of marbled murrelets in Owl Creek Grove. Subsequently, the judge determined that a permanent injunction barring Pacific Lumber's timber harvest plan was warranted.

Before the case was settled, Cowles had spent $200,000 of his own money to help EPIC, but it was worth it: The landmark decision sent a loud and clear message to private corporations that they were not above the law and would be held accountable for their transgressions on nature. The Owl Creek Grove Decision (as it was known) established the public's right to protect public assets such as endangered species—even on privately held lands.

The Public Bears Witness

Following an accident, Doug Riley-Thron traversed the forest on crutches to document the Thanksgiving Day Massacre on film. Disgusted with PL's illegal logging and the fact that all the government had done about it was to arrest some twenty activists who tried to stop the logging for the misdemeanor crime of trespassing, Riley-Thron knew he had to do more. So he dropped out of school and began spending his days in Headwaters. A skilled photographer, he began documenting both the mystic, timeless beauty of the ancient forest and its annihilation. And he took others into the old groves to bear witness, as he had. He taught his followers a variety of stealth tactics so they wouldn't be caught by the PL security guards who patrolled the property. "If anyone comes," he would say to his friend Joan Dunning, author of *From the Redwood Forest* (for which Riley-Thron shot the photographs), "go *downhill*, not up. You can't run fast enough uphill."

He also began contacting journalists, and some of the best followed him behind the Redwood Curtain to document the destruction of the last great redwood forest and its inhabitants. Soon Headwaters articles, along with Riley-Thron's photos, were appearing in *Time, People,* and *Glamour.* "I just knew if enough people could see this place, it would really make a difference," he says.

Doug Riley-Thron surveys the damage caused by clear-cutting the ancient Headwaters redwoods.

One morning in 1993, Riley-Thron answered a knock at his door and found a Pacific Lumber employee waving an envelope in his face. "It was a letter threatening to sue me if I didn't turn over all my slides and photos," Riley-Thron recalls. "PL also wanted a promise that I would never trespass into Headwaters again." He ignored the letter and continued to publish his photographs and show his slides. "The first show I ever did was here in Arcata. The city had charged me $100 for 'riot control,' so I was pretty nervous. But about 400 people came, and most of them were really into it. One woman, an apple farmer who had been supportive of the timber industry's property rights, really came around after seeing my aerial photographs. From the ground, she couldn't see the extent of the damage, but the slides changed her mind. She was really outspoken after that."

After a slide show in nearby Mendocino, a big, outgoing man approached Riley-Thron, introducing himself and his two children. Like Hurwitz, Ron Nadeau explained, he was a corporate man. His company, Grabber Performance Group, had made it big off air-activated hand warmers for cold-weather sports buffs. But Nadeau was dumbfounded by Hurwitz's unethical business practices. He told Riley-Thron to stay in touch; that the show had put fire in his belly. He wanted to see how he could help Riley-Thron and the others working to protect Headwaters. Shortly afterward, he sent Riley-Thron a phone card that paid for $2,000 worth of long-distance calls made to schedule slide shows across the nation. Riley-Thron didn't know it at the time, but Nadeau was also president of the Outdoor Industry Conservation Alliance (OICA), a group that gave money to causes like Headwaters.

Riley-Thron hit the road after the Mendocino show, living partly on his credit card and partly on handouts from folks who attended his presentations. He slept on any floor he could find. And he tirelessly asked people to write their lawmakers about Headwaters, for which protection was now embodied in northern California representative Dan Hamburg's Headwaters Forest Act. Meanwhile, Nadeau kept his promise to help by contacting the Headwaters Forest Coordinating Committee, later renamed the Headwaters Coalition. This impressive collection of groups had worked collaboratively since 1993 to save Headwaters. Each operated in its own niche, and together they ran the spectrum of styles and methods—from the dreadlocks of the Earth First!ers to the briefcases of the Sierra Club. Most of the groups were somewhere in between—made up of local residents.

From Ron Nadeau's perspective, the Headwaters Coalition groups stood like a stand of ancient redwoods. Each functioned as part of a whole, contributing to the synergy that fueled the entire system. Their strength was both in their numbers and in their wide range of tasks. It was the poetry of diversity.

Politicians in the Pockets of Industry

But despite all these citizen efforts, the redwoods were still vanishing at an alarming rate. In 1994 activists had looked to Representative Hamburg to pass a bill that effectively protected Headwaters from the saws of Hurwitz. With the help of citizens across the country and Riley-Thron's slide shows, the bill had gained the support of enough representatives to pass in the House, but it was axed in the Senate. Unfortunately, Hamburg was then ousted by Frank Riggs, an industry-supported conservative who was touting a legislative fix for the forest—but the fine print spelled the demise of the old trees and exempted Representative Riggs's corporate friends from the Endangered Species Act. And the Clinton administration had, as one coalition representative put it, "a pattern of pursuing politically driven compromises which combine the appearance of reform with Republican realities." It was getting difficult to know which battle to fight.

To complicate matters, U.S. senator Dianne Feinstein had thrown herself into the fray. A Democrat from California and supposed friend of the environment, Feinstein stood poised to take swift and bold action on behalf of Headwaters. The hopes of environmentalists everywhere soared—but to their dismay, Feinstein locked the greens out of the process while she personally negotiated with Hurwitz, who did real estate business with the senator's husband.

Conscience Companies Respond

Public outrage swept across the nation. Earth First! harnessed it in increasingly large demonstrations; September 15, 1996, marked the Carlotta Rally, which drew 8,000 people—a thousand of whom were arrested for civil disobedience. Ron Nadeau was there, as were five employees from Patagonia, a founding member of the Outdoor Industry Conservation Alliance. Patagonia had recently announced at its all-company meeting a new program in which it would pay its employees' bail fees if they were arrested in an act of nonviolent civil disobedience. John Sterling, who had recently come from Earth Island Institute to Patagonia's Environmental Affairs Department, was ready to take the company up on the offer. "It was a very civil affair," Sterling remembers. "The police were on their best behavior—which wasn't always the case at Headwaters demonstrations. They politely rounded us up, put us in buses, and dropped us out in the middle of nowhere. But Earth First! was so organized; they got a bunch of hippies to drive their vans out to our drop-off and shuttle us back to our cars."

By now, thanks to the public protests and EPIC's legal jousting, PL's clear-cutting had slowed. But it was a temporary change of pace; the company officials were merely biding their time until Feinstein's deal could be announced. The Headwaters Coalition groups scrambled. They realized that this was the moment to make a big push, before some irreversible decision was made.

It was time to start lobbying—and hard. The Riggs bill had to be stopped; the Clinton administration had to be persuaded to strengthen its stand; and Senator Feinstein needed to reconsider her dealings with Hurwitz before they were set in stone. All of this required a lot of political two-stepping—and that kind of activity could seriously jeopardize the nonprofit status of most of the coalition's groups. Furthermore, lobbying wasn't tax deductible, so funding for it was hard to come by.

Ron Nadeau had the answer for the Headwaters Coalition: Seek funding from the Outdoor Industry Conservation Alliance and run the money through a group with an unimpeachable tax status. At the next OICA board meeting, Patagonia and Grabber Performance Products put in profound pleas to their colleagues to help save Headwaters. The Alliance responded with $50,000— the only lobbying funds the coalition would receive during the campaign. Ron happily signed the check himself.

By October 1996 the Headwaters Coalition had money in the bank and folks on the road. Kate Crockett from the Trees Foundation was responsible for administering the funds—an impressive task given the number of groups and activists working on the issue. The first appropriations went to EPIC's Cecilia Lanman and Kevin Bundy, along with former congressional champion Dan Hamburg and California Sierra Clubber Kathy Bailey, to fly to D.C. and begin talks with the Clinton administration. The next chunk of change sent Darryl Cherney and other Earth First!ers to the Hurwitz savings-and-loan trial in Texas. There they assisted the federal attorneys with information they had gathered about the PL takeover while simultaneously coordinating public rallies to draw attention to Hurwitz, Maxxam, and PL.

More Betrayal

Meanwhile, Pacific Lumber's accumulated deeds were about to overwhelm the town of Stafford, California—literally. The steep hills above the town, owned by PL and fellow logging outfit Barnum Timber, heavily roaded and stripped of their trees, cut loose in the winter rains. On New Year's Eve, 1996, a massive mudslide hit the community, destroying half the town. PL refused to acknowledge any responsibility. At around the same time, the details of "The Deal" crafted by Feinstein and Hurwitz were beginning to go public. The Deal was devastating. As Kate Crockett put it, The Deal had been "masterminded behind closed doors in a smoke-filled room, without a single Headwaters Coalition representative." It approved budgeting $480 million plus a tax credit estimated as high as $600 million for acquisition of a meager portion of the 60,000-acre forest ecosystem. Furthermore, acquisition funding would be supplied by the state of California and the U.S. government—so taxpayers again would pay Hurwitz's debts. The PL plan did protect some additional acreage for fifty years, but that was nothing in terms of the lives of ancient trees. And to top it off, Hurwitz got an enormous tax break for writing the document.

But the darkest side of The Deal was the federal government's promise to approve Pacific Lumber's Habitat Conservation Plan (HCP)—a document that would permit PL to continue its logging practices throughout the rest of the forest. HCPs were conceived in an amendment to the Endangered Species Act; they allowed the exemption of small areas of habitat—not huge corporate holdings across an entire landscape—so that a landowner could conduct activities otherwise prohibited in endangered species' habitat. Nor do HCPs allow for adaptive management: When new species are listed, they will not be recognized under the HCP. From the mid-1980s until the Clinton administration took office, fewer than twenty HCPs were approved nationwide. More than 400 HCPs—with a new interpretation of "appropriate size" to include landscape scale—were approved after Clinton became president. In addition, the PL HCP came with an "incidental take permit" that allowed the company to "take" endangered species (that is, to kill endangered species or harm their habitat to the extent that it's no longer inhabitable by the species) on the rest of PL's land without any further review.

"I remember the senator's people calling me after The Deal went down," Riley-Thron says. "They wanted to buy my images of Headwaters, to give as gifts to the politicians who helped cut The Deal. I thought about sending them big photos of a clear-cut from the area they didn't bother to protect, but I just said, 'You couldn't pay me enough money to use my photos that way. You guys sold out.'"

Public Pressure Mounts

The recent political developments only fueled the coalition's efforts. More Conservation Alliance money was doled out so that citizens from all walks of life could fly to Washington and tell their stories to decision makers. Incidentally, Ron Nadeau got in his two cents as well—he had been called by Representative George Miller to testify before the House Natural Resources Committee on outdoor recreation industry issues. But Nadeau read the opportunity as a chance to make the case for Headwaters in front of an important captive audience.

Humboldt County residents, as well as activists from groups including EPIC, Earth First!, the Native American Coalition for Headwaters, and Taxpayers for Headwaters, were joined in Sacramento by citizens from the Bay Area under the umbrella of the Bay Area Coalition for Headwaters. The Conservation Alliance funds paid for such travel and lobby expenses—not one dime went toward salary or overhead. It was a different kind of effort than the California State Capitol had seen in 1991, when two Earth First! women, covered with nothing but mud, streaked across the Rotunda while two other activists rappelled from the capitol dome with a banner asking the politicians to save Headwaters.

Protesters in Arcata rally against the Headwaters Deal.

Despite the change in style, the 1997 lobby efforts were effective. Thousands of voices demanded that the state representatives either add protection to the Headwaters acquisition bill or kill it. The Clinton administration finally took notice and called for a special advisory council to work on the issue. Doug Riley-Thron, after much complaining about the lack of balance on the council, was able to sit at the table and push for protection of all 60,000 acres of Headwaters. A young man, an average citizen, had found his place among the politicians intent on compromises. Riley-Thron spoke for the trees, maintaining that the forest had already been compromised.

Death and Grief in the Village

But tragedy continued to flow through northern California. On March 2, 1997, Judi Bari died of breast cancer, and the entire community grieved. Rooted in Judi's spirit, Earth First!'s public actions continued full force, but the local police had become increasingly intolerant of any gathering in opposition to Pacific Lumber. In one demonstration activists dragged into Representative Riggs's office an ancient redwood stump. A group of young people sat around it, their arms locked and linked through metal pipe sleeves. Instead of ticketing the protestors, law enforcement officers yanked back their heads and swabbed their eyes with Q-Tips soaked in pepper spray—a technique used in several incidents. "This spray is supposed to be used to subdue violent criminals," one girl cried. "We are not violent criminals!" Another sobbed, "Don't you have a daughter?" while a third told the officers she was a teacher. An officer replied, "Well, you're gonna get a little education," as he doused her eyes with the caustic chemical.

But the most shocking incident came in 1998, when activist David "Gypsy" Chain was trying to halt a logging operation in Grizzly Creek near Headwaters, and an enraged logger felled a tree onto him. The blow crushed his skull, killing him instantly. Although environmentalists had warned the California Department of Forestry that PL was illegally logging in murrelet habitat, the department didn't send out an inspector until several days after the incident that took Gypsy's life. The inspector found that PL had once again violated the Endangered Species Act; Earth First! responded that "Gypsy died doing CDF's job."

Everything was at stake—the trees, the salmon, people's jobs, their drinking water, even their lives. Still, ordinary people continued to do extraordinary things: PL mill worker Doug Thomas quit his lumber job and began fighting for the redwoods. In a Humboldt County Board of Supervisors meeting, in front of his former peers and employers, Thomas pleaded with public officials to "stop the selling out of our children's legacy. There isn't much left. We can change. The salmon, they can't change."

Just a year earlier, a young preacher's daughter had climbed a lone-standing 1,500-year-old tree above the mud-covered town of Stafford. She was new to the West Coast but awestruck by the redwoods and overwhelmed by their demise. Julia "Butterfly" Hill had meant to stay in the tree for two weeks, but as she watched the clear-cutting continue around her, she vowed not to leave Luna, "her tree," until she could set foot in a world "where all of the remaining 3 percent of our ancient forests are protected forever." A village had formed beneath Luna—under the cover of night, Earth First! activists delivered food and words of encouragement before the security guards could catch them.

Months into her tree sit, Julia's immune system began to fail as did her resolve. Then one night a group of several hundred people arrived. After a thigh-burning uphill hike, the supporters circled Luna and began to beat drums and sing. They were led by Mickey Hart, the Grateful Dead's own legendary drummer. Hill found the strength to stay put, ultimately remaining in the tree for an amazing two years. Ducking helicopter harrassment, enduring El Niño storms and a ten-day starvation attempt by PL security, she came down only when Hurwitz finally agreed to protect the tree, along with a buffer zone around it, through a deed restriction.

For some, like Hill and Thomas—both tree huggers and tree cutters—the fight for the trees meant isolation from community. Others, happily, saw a strengthening of ties and a burgeoning of numbers. The rallies and protests for the redwoods continued to grow in number and popularity—celebrities like Woody Harrelson and Bonnie Raitt had long since raised their famous fists against Hurwitz and continued to draw crowds when they were called upon. And for Doug Riley-Thron, there was total unity: When Conservation Alliance funds enabled him to continue his slide show tour after his credit card was maxed out, he met his "activist soul mate," Karin Riley. A year later they would stand together beneath the ancient California redwoods and exchange wedding vows.

Sadly, after all the acts of courageous, collective protest, The Deal's final packaging was still a bitter insult to citizens who had worked so hard. Despite an entire nation of individuals, communities, and organizations—even other corporations—standing together in an attempt to protect the forest, elected representatives had struck a compromise that left most of Headwaters vulnerable to the insatiable saws of Charles Hurwitz.

Corporate Debt for Nature

The Deal may have been done, but activists didn't let it fly without clipping its wings. Government officials, feeling pressure from the public, yanked the Habitat Conservation Plan from the company's hands and rewrote it themselves. Some additional protection was garnered; while not strong enough to protect the forest in its entirety, the government's action demonstrated that corporations do not rule the nation and that the community—as well as the trees and the salmon—has rights that supersede private property rights.

Additionally, Hurwitz was feeling pressure from his Texas trial and the public ire directed toward him and his businesses. Thanks to the publicity given to the redwoods by the Headwaters Coalition groups, Rainforest Action Network launched a successful old-growth boycott that megachain Home Depot had sworn to honor. In a foretelling sign of defeat, Hurwitz's attorneys quietly entered into discussion with the feds about a "Debt for Nature" swap—*all* of Headwaters in exchange for the money he will owe if he is found guilty. The idea had been hatched by Darryl Cherney—the David to Hurwitz's Goliath—a scheme that ironically would keep Hurwitz out of jail.

The Power of the Village

In the words of Redwood Action Team's Darryl Cherney, "We don't even have a truce in the timber wars, let alone peace." Activists are still working tirelessly to ensure that Pacific Lumber's Deal-driven Habitat Conservation Plan is as strong as possible, through public comment and aggressive lobbying. If the HCP remains weak, the Headwaters Coalition has vowed to send it to its grave. And given the amount of public outrage the group has generated, there is little doubt that it can do just that.

Indeed, it takes a village. Perhaps many of them. Headwaters teaches us this: that we *can* fight the corporate world. The land may belong to PL, but citizens have a say about what PL does to the land if it imperils species, or pollutes our air or water. When Hurwitz and Maxxam took over Pacific Lumber, they submitted documents acknowledging that the property must be managed according to laws that protect species and govern forest management. And if our land managers won't enforce those laws, we the people can hold their feet to the fire.

But it takes the longhairs. The lawyers. The loggers. The young college students with cameras. It takes a collective of conscientious corporations—like the Conservation Alliance. It takes all of these—a poetry of diversity—to speak for the salmon, the streams, the ancient redwood trees. All of these voices, roots and limbs intertwined, stand together to outvote a single big business. It's a daunting task, an exercise in a grossly imbalanced democracy, but it can be done. And aren't the last great trees and all that depend on them worth it?

BIBLIOGRAPHY

Bari, Judi. *Timber Wars*. Monroe, Maine: Common Courage Press, 1994.

Cherney, Darryl, and Robert Parker. *Timber Wars Not Dead Yet: Headwaters Agreement Doesn't Effect [sic] Many Other Battles with Maxxam/PL*. www.jailhurwitz.com, Luna Media Services, 1999.

"Company Accepts Forest Pact: U.S., California, Offer Maxxam $380 Million in Land, Cash." *Dallas Morning News*, 29 September 1996, 13A.

Dunning, Joan. *From the Redwood Forest: Ancient Trees and the Bottom Line: A Headwaters Journey*. White River Junction, Vt.: Chelsea Green Publishing, 1998.

Earth First! Worker Outreach Project. *Headwaters Forest Stewardship or . . . The Deal?* Redway, Calif.: Earth First! Worker Outreach Project, 1999.

Environmentally Sound Promotions. *Headwaters Forest Fact Sheet*. Redway, Calif.: Environmentally Sound Promotions, 1998.

Fire in the Eyes. Produced and directed by James Ficklin. 32 min. Headwaters Action Video Collective, 1999. Videocassette.

Harris, David. *The Last Stand: The War Between Wall Street and Main Street Over California's Ancient Redwoods*. San Francisco: Sierra Club Books, 1996.

Headwaters Forest Coordinating Committee. *The Headwaters Lobbying Campaign: A Proposal to the Outdoor Industry Conservation Alliance*. Redway, Calif.: Trees Foundation, 1996.

Skow, John. "Redwoods: The Last Stand, A Young Activist Fights a Corporate Raider to Save an Ancient California Forest from Being Cut Down." *Time*, 6 June 1994, 58.

Trees Foundation. *The Headwaters Forest Stewardship Plan: A Citizens' Alternative to Maxxam Management of Headwaters Forest.* Redway, Calif.: Trees Foundation, producer, 1997.

————. *Headwaters Forest Update.* Redway, Calif.: Trees Foundation, summer 1999.

Voices of Humboldt County: The Cumulative Impact. Produced and directed by Salmon Forever. 55 min. 1997. Videocassette.

Walker, Blair S. "Takeover Artist Ruthless, Philanthropic." *USA Today,* 29 July 1992, B2.

Zakin, Susan. *Coyotes and Town Dogs: Earth First and the Environmental Movement.* New York: Penguin Books, 1993.

Breaking the Mold

Alberton Gorge, Montana
1986–2000

"America is a great story, and there is a river on every page of it."

—*Charles Kuralt*

This country loves a good tale. Especially one with a happy ending—where the dragon is slain and the village saved and everyone lives happily ever after. But how often does real life have that kind of fairy-tale finale? Indeed, they're rare. But in the tale of saving an immaculate stretch of Montana's Clark Fork River, there are simply good guys and good vibes from beginning to end. And it's a tale worth telling—precisely because its archetypes are atypical.

Take the story's environmentalists. Most folks out West think of environmentalists as "East Coast elitists"—in other words, latté-lapping Manhattanites who don't know the difference between a pronghorn and a longhorn. Or even a sagebrush and a hairbrush.

Surely those folks haven't met Peter Dayton. Or Art Neill. Born under the big sky of Montana, raised paddling and fishing its rivers and walking across its wide-open spaces, both men are living proof that even homegrown westerners can have green souls. At first glance Peter Dayton wouldn't seem like a do-gooder for the earth. After all, he's a real estate attorney. And Neill worked for forty years for Montana Power and its mining subsidiary, Western Energy.

Then there are the corporations. The greens usually pull their swords from their scabbards when a big company comes on the

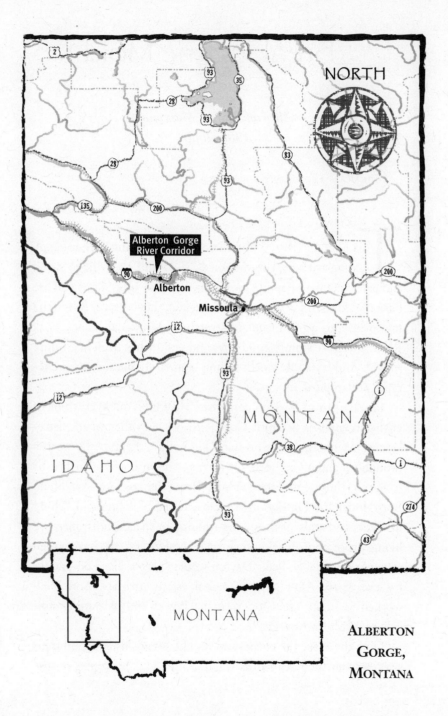

NORTH

Alberton Gorge
River Corridor

Alberton

Missoula

MONTANA

IDAHO

MONTANA

**ALBERTON
GORGE,
MONTANA**

scene, saying that big biz is the dragon that pillages the village—and the land and water around it. And the greens add a complaint against industry's unwieldy sense of *entitlement*.

But in the case of Alberton Gorge, Montana Power escaped the corporate cliché, and Peter Dayton and Art Neill ducked the stereotypes of professional men. Montana Power did its best—especially for a dam-building, mineral-mining operation. It was reclaiming surface mines long before the government said it had to and getting national recognition for doing a good job. And even before the gorge project, Dayton and Neill were spreading green fairy dust across the state: Dayton was helping groups like the Rocky Mountain Elk Foundation put private properties into conservation easements, and Neill was serving on the Montana board of trustees of The Nature Conservancy (TNC). So there was a fine cast of characters before the story even got rolling.

A Boating Haven

High on the Continental Divide, the Clark Fork River is born—the largest river in the northern Rockies. Not much of this river remains untainted by humans. It has been diverted for power and farms, and served as a receptacle for mining and industrial poisons. Dams dot its course like braces on teeth. And the more scenic stretches have been blighted by trophy homes and pseudocabins the size of castles—attempts to live the great western dream.

Along its 320-mile route, the river flows west through Missoula and then plummets into Alberton Gorge, a steep chasm lined with ancient, violet-colored stone. There the Clark Fork transforms into seven miles of writhing, roiling white water—a favorite stretch among western kayakers and rafters, especially at low water, when other rivers run out of steam. It is the home of the Montana Whitewater Championships, where boats literally cartwheel atop mischievous waves, racking up points for style and difficulty along the way. "The access is incredible," said competitive kayaker Seth Warren in a recent interview with the *Missoulian*.

"The spot is beautiful and there's great viewing from the bridge." Indeed, most folks only ever saw the gorge from the bridge, one of the few man-made structures in sight.

It was the remote feeling of the gorge—despite being hemmed in by a highway and railroad only 30 miles from Missoula—that wove kayakers into its fate. Once upon a time in the mid-1970s, local Boy Scout leader Ralph Yule, who was already nearing his fiftieth birthday, took up boating. Mastering the most unwieldy waves in the gorge meant smashing up a lot of boats—which Yule made in his garage from a plastic mold.

Yule had a boating partner who had lost a leg. The man had tremendous difficulty at the Fish Creek takeout, which was a long and grueling uphill trudge. It was also very dangerous. At one point the trail crossed the railroad tracks at a blind corner; several boaters—bogged down with their boats and deafened by the roar of the river—had nearly been taken out by oncoming trains. Concerned with his friend's needs and the safety of the entire community, Yule took it upon himself to scout every inch of the gorge for an exit. He found a perfect one—but it was on private property owned by Montana Power. So the eccentric boatbuilder formed a group, the Missoula Whitewater Association, and organized it to purchase the new access from the power company. In gratitude the locals named the new spot Ralph's Take-Out.

By the time Ralph was in his seventies, he was learning to tele-mark ski and running rivers all over the West. Still, he complained that he was getting up there in age. Soon Ralph announced his idea to bulldoze a road down to the takeout. He began to lean on Montana Power to do so.

Preservation Before Recreation

Enter Peter Dayton, the real estate attorney. A passionate boater known for sliding his kayak down miles of snowy mountain slopes to reach inaccessible white water in the spring, Dayton was famil-iar with the goings-on in the gorge. "As sympathetic as we were to Ralph's limitations, we knew that environmentally, 'dozing a road down there was a really bad idea. So we went to Montana Power and said, 'Please don't let old Ralph do this.'" The conversation marked the beginning of Peter Dayton's relationship with Montana Power and Art Neill, who at the time was serving as executive vice president for the company.

Looking Ahead

The Missoula Whitewater Association was mostly one dimensional, a storefront to lend credibility to Ralph's access efforts. But over time, as other boaters like Peter Dayton got involved, the group grew some muscle. Soon they found themselves talking about the trouble they saw looming before Alberton Gorge. "We were worried about property development on the river," Dayton recalls. "Real estate was booming in Montana, and the gorge was prime riverfront property. I could just imagine it becoming littered with balconies, patios, gazebos, and lawns. There's only so much river. We thought we better figure out how to protect this one piece."

Dayton went to the courthouse to find out who owned the properties along the river's seven-mile stretch through the gorge. "I feared there would be dozens of individually owned parcels to deal with," he recalls. He was in luck. The boaters' new friend, Montana Power, owned two-thirds of the best white-water stretch. The company had purchased it in the 1930s, thinking it would build a hydrodam and reservoir there. The idea was revisited several times over the next decades, but the economic stars had failed to align and the facility was never constructed. "The gorge property was just sitting on their books as surplus," says Dayton.

He contacted Art Neill for a face-to-face meeting, and was pleased to discover that they shared the same green glimmer in their eyes. As Dayton explained his concerns about Alberton Gorge, Neill nodded his head in total comprehension—an unusual response for a corporate executive talking about environmental stuff. But Neill understood ecosystems, and the significance of river corridors within those systems. Neill's schooling in these matters had really taken off in the 1980s, when he began rubbing elbows with John Sawhill, the president of the national Nature Conservancy. (Sawhill has since died of diabetes complications.) After a backpacking trip with the conservation leader, Neill decided that Montana Power should "do the right thing" and become a corporate supporter of TNC's efforts in Montana. He met no resistance from his superiors or the board of directors. "I definitely wasn't a voice in the wilderness on that decision," Neill

The roiling white water of the Clark Fork River through Alberton Gorge is a favorite among kayakers and rafters.

says proudly. Shortly afterward the power company donated to the conservation group a surplus ranch property—which, by prior agreement, TNC turned around and sold for cash to support a key conservation acquisition. Soon Neill found himself on TNC's Montana board of trustees, providing time and money—both his own and the company's—in an effort to further the group's mission to protect permanently large tracts of private land.

Neill knew Dayton was right. "I could see that the situation in the gorge was going to get worse instead of better," Neill says. "More and more, developers were approaching us about putting our property on the market." Without hesitation, Neill agreed to join Dayton and his colleagues on a float trip for a close-up view of the gorge.

An avid canoer who loved to fly fish, Neill was predictably seduced by the deep slice of earth, white sandy beaches, and vivacious waters that made up the gorge. Dayton pointed out how the river corridor provided a crucial crossing for big-game animals traveling between the Ninemile Range and the Bitterroot Mountains. He showed Neill where the eagles and ospreys nested, and where vacation homes were cropping up above and below the narrow stretch.

If there had ever been any question in Neill's mind, there wasn't anymore. He knew the gorge had to be left just as it was—undeveloped and thriving with the wilderness experience that itself was becoming an endangered species. "I knew the Clark Fork and I knew there weren't too many stretches left like that one," he says.

Mutual Respect

Dayton was wowed by Neill's deftness with environmental issues—for a guy who ordered dams built and minerals mined, he was downright impressive. And his commitment to doing the right thing was so genuine. Neill felt the same way about Dayton; here was a real estate lawyer who saw in the gorge habitat and scenery and public enjoyment—rather than subdivisions and fat commission checks.

Right there, Neill promised Dayton that Montana Power wouldn't sell off the gorge property right away—that he'd talk to the company officials and stockholders and see what they could do to help protect it. It was a generous offer—considering that the pricetag on the property was more than a million bucks. Besides, it would have been easier just to unload it on the market and be done with it. Art knew that his commitment meant some long-term wheeling and dealing, but the company had been down this road before—opting to get land into a protective arrangement rather than hastily developing it.

That was in 1989. The boating community, along with local outfitters and anglers, started looking for private donors to buy up the land and put it into a conservation easement. "Poor Montana Power," Dayton sighs. "They were so patient with us, and we were like mosquitoes buzzing in their ears, constantly bothering them while we tried every trick in our bag to buy the stretch on the river. But nothing worked out."

Despite Montana Power's patience, the involved citizens were beginning to feel a sense of urgency. As the national energy situation evolved, so would Montana Power. Dayton and others feared that the company would be bought out by a less accommodating owner, and the gorge would either be dammed or be sold for development.

Into the Labyrinth

What followed was months of attempted land exchanges—the first being a simple swap between Montana Power and the Forest Service. When that fell through, the mix was spiced up with more land and more players. The negotiations dragged on. Bruce Bugbee, the best-respected land acquisition consultant in Montana, was hired by Montana Power to help with the process. An easygoing person with a knack for building solid relationships, Bugbee gained Neill's and everyone else's trust immediately. So when Bugbee said they needed a third-party nonprofit group to play middleman in the deal, everyone went along with his suggestion.

Most of the players already knew Hugh Zackheim. He had been in Montana for years, working with The Nature Conservancy and other groups. Now he was the northern Rockies director for The River Conservancy, an acquisition program of River Network, a group formed to help citizens understand, protect, and restore rivers and watersheds across the nation. Zackheim was on the project immediately the way he was onto a good poker game, and soon River Network was sculpting a $50,000 option to buy. The option agreement would give the parties the time they needed to arrange the land exchange and come up with enough cash to buy out Montana Power.

As Northwest director for The River Conservancy, Zackheim's colleague Sue Doroff was in charge of finding the funds to make the purchase option a go. Doroff immediately thought of Perception Kayaks, a small but impressively active company within the Outdoor Industry Conservation Alliance (OICA). At the time, boater Risa Shimoda Callaway was representing Perception on the Alliance board. Doroff knew that Callaway was one of the most engaged individuals to ever serve the board; her track record for getting Perception's pet projects funded was 100 percent. What's more, Callaway had a small but sweet personal connection to River Network: Years before, the wife of one of its directors had taught her to Eskimo roll in a kayak.

Now Callaway was boating up a storm and had founded the National Organization of Whitewater Rodeos. With the same vitality she displayed on the river, she took on River Network's proposal to the Alliance as if it were her own. "I felt really badly, though," she says. "I made them rewrite their proposal. It's just that I wanted it to be perfect, so it would get the votes needed for funding."

Ultimately, the outdoor industry was like the knight in shining armor that rode in to save Alberton Gorge. The option to buy was financed by a $35,000 grant from the Conservation Alliance and one for $15,000 from American Whitewater. These two sources of funding kept the land off the market and gave the groups the time they needed to work out the particulars on the exchange.

By early 1999, with River Network at the helm, a four-way swap was finally announced to the public—between the U.S. Forest Service, Montana Power, River Network, and the Montana

Department of Fish, Wildlife, and Parks (FWP). The swap looked like a win-win situation for Montana Power's stockholders, for the agencies, and for the public. The local papers sang the praises of the partnership. The folks who had been at the table for the past few years beamed with satisfaction and pointed to one another, not themselves, as the reason for the project's success. Zackheim said it was Peter Dayton's efforts—evidenced in his thorough and tireless review of a "monumentally complex, three-inch-thick title policy." Peter Dayton gave credit where he saw credit due; he told Sherry Devlin, a Missoula reporter, that River Network had been the "fairy godmother" of the deal. And he said later that "Bruce Bugbee and Hugh Zackheim glued this thing together for us." But he couldn't say enough good things about Montana Power, either, noting that Art Neill especially had provided vision for the project. And he was impressed by the agencies' roles, and especially by the Department of Fish, Wildlife and Parks for doing some incredible gymnastics to make the exchange successful. It seemed a happy story all the way around.

Economic Realities

There was one glitch, but it wasn't because of a fire-breathing beast with malevolent intent. Nearby Mineral County was having a rough time with the deal—and understandably so. Approximately 90 percent of the land within its boundaries was already publicly owned, and residents didn't feel that they could afford more land going into the public coffers. For a small rural county, losing a potential development property with its prospect for future tax revenue would be a pretty big blow. And county officials could already hear the numbers crunching for bridge and road repairs above their part of the gorge—as well as river rescues. The county commissioners pointed to the fact that most of the 30,000 visitors who were coming annually to the gorge purchased supplies in Missoula County. They'd boat the river and then leave without spending a dime over the county line. Why should Mineral

County clean up after them without getting a little cream from the deal?

The land-swap partners didn't really need Mineral County's blessing—its residents might complain during the public comment period, but they probably wouldn't make enough noise to derail the synergy among the negotiating parties and Missoula County residents. But nobody wanted to be the archfiend. So it was back to the table to reconfigure the exchange in a way that would work for Mineral County.

The deadline for the purchase option was nearing, and River Network had to move fast. The organization committed another $50,000—this time using its own funds to support the previous year's contributions from the Conservation Alliance and American Whitewater. The option to buy the property was extended through December 2000, to work out the kinks—both with Mineral County and with the sluggish environmental review process that the agencies were pursuing under state and federal requirements. Still, it was a lot of money to pay for something as intangible as time.

In March 2000 the *Missoulian* unveiled the details of the proposed exchange, newly crafted to satisfy the concerns expressed by Mineral County. When the deal is said and done, River Network's River Conservancy will purchase the Montana Power property in Alberton Gorge for somewhat more than a million dollars, and then transfer it to the Department of Fish, Wildlife, and Parks to manage for the public. FWP will in turn trade several parcels of state property to the Forest Service—mostly public fishing access points surrounded by national forest lands. The Forest Service will then provide River Network with about 300 acres of land in Mineral County that the group will sell to cover its expenditures in purchasing Alberton Gorge. The needs of the county will be accommodated by sale of this property into private ownership, stimulating tax revenue for the concerned county.

On Independence Day 2000 the *Missoulian* publicized an

upcoming series of local hearings at which FWP would discuss the details of the proposal and take public comments on the exchange. Lee Bastian, regional parks manager for FWP, was extremely helpful in making the exchange a reality. He was quoted as saying, "The opportunity is now. If we don't do something now to try and protect Alberton Gorge from development, it will be another piece of Montana that is lost." The public hearings were wrapped up by midsummer, passing with little contention. By 2001 everyone can confidently expect to see Alberton Gorge enter the public domain to remain in its raw and natural state for generations to come.

Every Bit of River Counts

The story of protecting the gorge really seems too good to be true—as far as true-life stories of environmental protection go. All good guys, all good intentions.

Perhaps the dragon is in the larger story of American rivers: Less than one-quarter of 1 percent of them is protected with Wild and Scenic status. Of the 1,200 species listed as threatened or endangered, 50 percent depend on rivers and streams for their survival. And 70 percent of riparian habitat has been lost or altered nationwide.

Saving Alberton Gorge becomes an even happier tale against a backdrop of such sobering information. Montana Power seems an even more extraordinary corporation, and Neill and Dayton appear all the more heroic. Had these archetypal characters stuck to their stereotypes, had they done "business as usual" as so many real estate and corporate men do, this would have been a morbid horror film rather than a happily ever after.

BIBLIOGRAPHY

Cohen, Betsy. "Organizers Seek Higher Profile for Montana Whitewater Championships." *Missoulian*, 15 May 2000.

Devlin, Sherry. "A Kindly Teacher, Outdoor Lover Passes." *Missoulian*, 27 December 1998.

———. "FWP Makes Deal to Protect River Corridor." *Missoulian*, 23 March 2000.

———. "The Gorge – Forever." *Missoulian*, 8 March 1999.

———. "Testing Waters." *Missoulian*, 4 July 2000.

Doroff, Sue. "Conservation Alliance Request for Proposal, 1997." Portland, Ore.: River Network. Photocopy.

River Conservancy. *The Campaign for Western Rivers: Creating the River Protection Fund*. Portland, Ore.: River Network, 1998.

How You Can Make a Difference

Lasting environmental change happens at the grassroots level, when people become stewards of the land and the species around them and actively participate in their protection. There are many ways to raise your voice. The following is a tool kit of resources designed to help you take the first step toward protecting our shared environment.

Volunteer

One of the most effective ways to protect the environment is to volunteer for a group working on an environmental cause that is important to you. Get in touch with Conservation Alliance grant recipients and let them know you'd like to help. (See Appendix i for information on contacting some of the groups you've read about in this book.) There are likely several environmental groups in your community that would love your assistance. Contact them to find out how you can support their important work.

Letter-Writing Campaigns

It's important that elected officials hear from us. Our representatives create and implement the policies that impact the health of our environment. We can't expect them to properly represent us if we don't let them know what we think. Send a postcard, fax, or digital petition, or make a phone call. None of these compare, however, with the power of a handwritten letter.

Helpful hints when writing your representative:
- Keep it simple. Limit your letter to a couple of concise paragraphs focused on one specific issue. Ask for specific action

from your elected official, either to support or oppose the measure. Include the name and bill number of the legislation.

- Make it personal. Remember, our governing bodies are there to represent the people. Let them know why this issue is important to you and your community.
- Ask for a reply. Include your name and address on both the letter and the envelope.
- Thank your elected officials when appropriate.

Letters to the Editor

Letters to the editor are one of the most widely read sections of a local newspaper. They allow community members to comment on the way issues are being presented in the paper, and they encourage the paper to cover issues its editors may have thought were insignificant to the community. These letters are a fantastic way to raise awareness on important issues in your community. Newspapers don't run every letter they receive. Before you write your opinion, spend some time reading the letters that have been printed. The guidelines for letters and where to send them will sometimes be listed on the editorial page.

The more letters the newspaper receives on a specific subject, the better the chance that at least one of them will be printed. Your letter will most likely be edited. Here are a few suggestions to make your letter more appealing: Keep it short and concise. If you're responding to an article that previously appeared in the paper, include the headline and day the article ran. Use language that will engage the reader. Choose words that show emotion. Be factual. Be sure to highlight aspects of the issue that have not been previously addressed. When possible, type your letter. When sending copies to multiple newspapers, individually sign each letter. Address envelopes by hand.

Public Hearings

Public hearings are usually scheduled just before a city votes on a particular project or a state agency is about to take action. Regardless of whether or not the hearing will directly affect a vote, it's important that the community participate. The number of people allowed to speak at hearings is usually limited because of time constraints. In most cases there will be a sign-up sheet posted at the hearing site. Arrive at the location early to ensure a better chance of speaking. Each speaker is given a time limit for comments. Make sure to limit the points you raise to those you feel are most important. In most cases folks are encouraged to also submit written statements. This provides the opportunity to raise additional concerns.

Be polite. Public hearings are a place for people representing both sides of an issue to address concerns in a public format. It is important to show respect for all sides of the issue, regardless whether or not you personally agree. Public hearings are a great way to generate media coverage for an issue. When appropriate, bring signs and placards to help convey your message.

Environmental Activism Checklist

- Volunteer
- Write letters
- Provide public hearing testimony
- Vote
- Shop selectively
- Participate in boycotts
- Reduce or change personal consumption
- Make financial contributions to non-profit environmental groups

These are just a few of the ways to get involved in your local community; many others exist. The most important thing is to get involved—period. The Conservation Alliance agrees with the Quaker idea of bearing witness: If you see an injustice, you are obligated to act to correct it. If you aren't part of the solution, you're part of the problem. We hope that you'll join us in our efforts to reduce the environmental impacts we all have on the earth.

John Sterling
Director of Environmental Programs
Patagonia, Inc.

Appendix i

Contact Information

To find out how you can help some of the causes you've read about here, contact one or more of the following groups:

Idaho Rivers

Wendy L. Wilson
River Network
3920 Twilight Court
Boise, ID 83703
(208) 345–3689; fax: (208) 345–1588
wlw@micron.net

Idaho Rivers United (has replaced Friends of the Payette)
P.O. Box 633
Boise, ID 83701
(208) 343–7481; fax: (208) 343–9376
bsedivy@idahorivers.org
www.idahorivers.org

The Dugout Ranch, Southern Utah

The Nature Conservancy of Utah
559 East South Temple
Salt Lake City, UT 84102
(801) 531–0999; fax: (801) 531–1003
www.tnc.org

Tatshenshini River Campaign

BC Spaces for Nature
P.O. Box 673
Gibson, British Columbia V0N 1V0
Canada

(604) 886–8605; fax: (604) 886–3768
bcspaces@spacesfornature.org
www.spacesfornature.org

The Shawangunks Land Purchase

The Access Fund
P.O. Box 17010
Boulder, CO 80308
(303) 545–6772; fax: (303) 545–6774
info@accessfund.org
www.accessfund.org

Mohonk Preserve, Inc.
P.O. Box 715
New Paltz, NY 12561-0715
(845) 255–0919; fax: (845) 255–5646
mpglennh@idsi.net
www.mohonkpreserve.org

Friends of the Shawangunks
P.O. Box 270
Accord, NY 12404
(845) 687–4759
gunks@hotmail.com
www.nynjtc.org

InterTribal Sinkyone Wilderness Council, California

P.O. Box 1523
Ukiah, CA 95482
(707) 463–6745

South Yuba River Campaign, California

South Yuba River Citizens League
216 Main Street
Nevada City, CA 95959
(530) 265–5961; fax: (530) 265–6232
www.syrcl.org

Texas Sea Turtle Campaign
HEART (Help Endangered Animals–Ridley Turtles)
P.O. Box 681231
Houston, TX 77268-1231
Phone/fax: (281) 444–6204
www.ridleyturtles.org

Sea Turtle Restoration Project/Turtle Island Restoration
Network
P. O. Box 400
(415) 488–0370; fax: (415) 488–0372
seaturtles@igc.org
www.seaturtles.org

New World Mine Campaign, Montana
The Park County Environmental Council (has replaced the
Beartooth Alliance)
P.O. Box 164
Livingston, MT 59047
(406) 222–0723
envirocouncil@imt.net

Greater Yellowstone Coalition
P.O. Box 1874
Bozeman, MT 59771
(406) 586–1593
gyc@greateryellowstone.org

Clavey River, California
Tuolumne River Preservation Trust
Fort Mason Building C
San Francisco, CA 94123
(415) 292–3531; fax: (415) 931–1813

Tuolumne River Preservation Trust
914 13th Street
Modesto, CA 95354
(209) 236–0330; fax: (209) 236–0311
staff@tuolumne.org
www.tuolumne.org

Clavey River Preservation Coalition
c/o Glenda Edwards
17860 Wards Ferry Road
Sonora, CA 95370
(209) 532–7110; fax: (209) 536–0876
gedwards@inreach.com

RESTORE: The North Woods, Maine

RESTORE: The North Woods
P.O. Box 1099
West Concord, MA 01742
(978) 287–0320; fax: (978) 287–5771
restore@restore.org
www.restore.org

Headwaters Forest Campaign, California

Trees Foundation
P.O. Box 2202
Redway, CA 95560
(707) 923–4377
trees@igc.org
www.treesfoundation.org

Environmental Protection Information Center (EPIC)
P.O. Box 397
Garberville, CA 95542
(707) 923–2931
www.igc.apc.org

Doug Riley-Thron
Thron Nature Photography
P.O. Box 703
Arcata, CA 95518
(707) 822–4870
newriverwild@hotmail.com
www.turquoiseriver.com.

Rose Foundation for Communities and the Environment
6008 College Avenue, Suite 10
Oakland, CA 94618
(510) 658–0702; fax: (510) 658–0732
rosefdn@earthlink.net

North Coast Earth First!
P.O. Box 28
Arcata, CA 95518
(707) 825–6598
ncef@humboldt1.com

Mattole Forest Defenders
P.O. Box 28
Arcata, CA 95518
(707) 441–3828
www.mattoledefense.org

Montana Rivers

River Network (headquarters)
520 Sixth Avenue SW
Portland, OR 97204
(503) 241–3506
www.rivernetwork.org

River Network
Northern Rockies Office
44 North Last Chance Gulch
Helena, MT 59601
(406) 442–4777
montanazac@aol.com

National Organizations that Support Local Grassroots Efforts

The Humane Society of the United States
2100 L Street, NW
Washington, DC 20037
www.hsus.org

Natural Resources Defense Council
40 West 20th Street
New York, NY 10011
(212) 727–2700; fax: (212) 727–1773
nrdcinfo@nrdc.org
www.nrdc.org

National Audubon Society
700 Broadway
New York, NY 10003
(212) 979–3000; fax: (212) 979–3188
www.audubon.org

The Nature Conservancy
4245 North Fairfax Drive, Suite 100
Arlington, VA 22203-1606
(800) 628–6860
www.tnc.org

Rainforest Action Network
221 Pine Street, Suite 500
San Francisco, CA 94104
(415) 398–4404; fax: (415) 398–2732
www.ran.org

Sierra Club
85 Second Street, Second Floor
San Francisco, CA 94105-3441
(415) 977–5500; fax: (415) 977–5799
www.sierraclub.org

The Wilderness Society
1615 M Street, NW
Washington, DC 20036
(800) 843–9453
www.wilderness.org

Appendix ii

Conservation Alliance Grants
December 1988–November 2000

The Conservation Alliance is a group of outdoor businesses whose collective contributions support grassroots citizen-action groups and their efforts to protect wild and natural areas where outdoor enthusiasts recreate. Alliance funds have played a pivotal role in the protection of rivers, trails, wild lands, and climbing areas for muscle-powered recreation.

Year Given	Organization Project
1989	**Friends of the Payette** (Idaho) *Project:* To protect the North Fork of Idaho's Payette River.
1989	**Appalachian Trail Conference** (West Virginia) *Project:* To acquire lands bordering the Appalachian Trail corridor with the goal of creating a greenbelt bordering the footpath.
1989	**Greater Yellowstone Coalition** (Montana) *Project:* To protect the Snake River Watershed, a vital part of the Greater Yellowstone ecosystem.
1989	**The Utah Wilderness Coalition** (Utah) *Project:* To protect 5.1 million acres of public lands in Utah's canyon and desert region.

1990   **Natural Resources Council of Maine** (Maine)
            Project: To protect the recreational resources in
            Maine's North Woods region, which faces pres-
            sure from nearby development.

1990   **Friends of the Shawangunks** (New York)
            Project: To acquire lands in New York's
            Shawangunks for protection from encroaching
            suburban development.

1990   **Friends of the River** (California)
            Project: To protect the environmental and recre-
            ational resources of the Colorado River in the
            Grand Canyon.

1990   **West Virginia Rivers Coalition**
            (Washington, D.C.)
            Project: To seek protection of 12 river segments
            in Monogahela National Forest.

1990   **Trust for Public Land/Pinnacles Fund**
            (Washington)
            Project: To help make Peshastin Pinnacles a
            Washington State Park for climbing.

1990   **Ice Age Park and Trail** (Wisconsin)
            Project: To organize grassroots volunteers to
            complete and maintain the Wisconsin Ice Age
            National Scenic Trail.

1991   **The Oregon Rivers Council** (Oregon)
            Project: To encourage institution of the
            Northwest Hydropower and Renewable Energy
            Project.

1991   **Tatshenshini Wild** (British Columbia)
            Project: To help protect the Tatshenshini River of
            The Yukon, British Columbia, and Alaska.

1991   **The Green Mountain Club** (Vermont)
Project: To help acquire 38 miles of the Long
Trail in northern Vermont.

1991   **Smith River Alliance** (California)
Project: To help shape implementation of the
Smith River National Recreation Area Act, and
ensure protection of this California river and its
watershed.

1991   **Western Ancient Forest Campaign** (Oregon)
Project: To help protect the ancient forests of
California, Oregon, and Washington.

1991   **Northeast Alliance to Protect James Bay**
(Massachusetts)
Project: To help protect Canada's James and
Hudson Bays in Quebec from the impact of
hydroelectric development.

1991   **Share the Water Coalition** (California)
Project: To support federal water reform to protect California's San Francisco Bay/Delta estuary
and Central Valley.

1992   **Idaho Rivers United** (Idaho)
Project: To gain permanent protection for 80
free-flowing rivers in Idaho.

1992   **Inland Empire Public Lands Council**
(Washington)
Project: To support Forest Watch, a program
designed to empower citizens to influence
Northwest national forest management.

1992   **Friends of the River** (California)
Project: To protect California's American River
from proposed dam projects.

1992	**Friends of Grandfather Mountain** (North Carolina) *Project:* To protect North Carolina's Grandfather Mountain and enhance its recreational resources.
1992	**Lighthawk, The Environmental Air Force** (New Mexico) *Project:* To monitor forest management in the Pacific Northwest and raise public awareness of the threats facing the region's recreational resources.
1992	**The Southern Utah Wilderness Alliance** (Utah) *Project:* To build grassroots support for the protection of Utah's Virgin River Basin.
1992	**River Conservation International** (Washington, D.C.) *Project:* To protect Chile's Bio Bio River, one of the world's wildest rivers, from hydropower development.
1993	**Adirondack Mountain Club** (New York) *Project:* To expand its volunteer and professional trail maintenance program.
1993	**The Access Fund** (Colorado) *Project:* To purchase a 40-acre parcel in New York's Near-Trapps area that will help keep this popular recreation site open to the public.
1993	**The Sierra Club of Western Canada** (British Columbia) *Project:* To produce public education materials

and coordinate an awareness campaign to gain protection for the Clayoquot Sound area.

1993   **The Oregon Natural Resources Council** (Oregon)
Project: To build public support and influence policy-makers to halt or remove 12 specified dams in Oregon.

1993   **American Whitewater Affiliation** (Maryland)
Project: To implement a plan to improve recreational access to the nation's whitewater rivers and streams.

1993   **Mineral Policy Center** (Washington, D.C.)
Project: To launch a lobbying campaign to reform the 1872 Mining Law to protect the nation's recreational lands from mining's impacts.

1993   **Forests Forever, Inc.** (California)
Project: To implement a public education, legislative and electoral campaign to protect Northern California's largest remaining unprotected virgin redwood grove.

1993   **Friends of the Bitterroot** (Montana)
Project: To lobby state and national legislators for Wilderness designation of unprotected wildlands in Idaho and Montana's Bitterroot Valley area.

1993   **InterTribal Sinkyone Wilderness Council** (California)
Project: To purchase 3,800 acres of land in Mendocino County to establish the nation's first InterTribal Wilderness Park.

1994   **Trout Unlimited** (Virginia)
            Project: To fund a grassroots campaign to protect
            and enhance local streams to support salmon.

1994   **Tuolumne River Preservation Trust**
            (California)
            Project: To protect the Clavey River from a dam.

1994   **Greater Yellowstone Coalition** (Montana)
            Project: To protect the Yellowstone Ecosystem by
            defeating the establishment of a mine that would
            affect the region and its rivers.

1994   **Sierran Biodiversity Institute** (California)
            Project: To protect Sierra forests by mapping,
            with information widely used by grassroots
            groups.

1994   **Pinelands Preservation Alliance** (New Jersey)
            Project: To protect the New Jersey Pinelands for
            recreation.

1994   **Mississippi River Basin Alliance** (Missouri)
            Project: First citizen awareness campaign to pro-
            tect the Mississippi River.

1994   **Northwoods Wilderness Recovery** (Michigan)
            Project: To develop and promote a new forest
            management plan to support wild lands recovery
            in Michigan's Upper Peninsula and northeastern
            Wisconsin.

1994   **New York-New Jersey Trail Conference**
            (New York)
            Project: For a public education and lobbying
            effort aimed at securing funds for the protection
            and acquisition of 20,000 acres of forest land,

which the group says is home to 1,100 miles of
recreation trails.

1994   **South Yuba River Citizens League**
         (California)
         Project: To implement a citizen-action campaign
         to get California's South Yuba River included in
         the Wild & Scenic River Systems and to secure
         permanent protection for this free-flowing river.

1994   **Road Removal Implementation Project**
         (California)
         Project: To develop training materials to assist
         citizens in advocating for the restoration and
         preservation of unused roads on wild lands
         across the nation.

1995   **Heartwood** (Indiana)
         Project: To coordinate citizen efforts to encour-
         age the establishment of an extensive wilderness
         preserve throughout the Central Appalachians.

1995   **Montana River Action Network** (Montana)
         Project: To organize grassroots support through-
         out Montana to prevent a new rivers' designa-
         tion that MRAN says will weaken the state's
         water quality and allow for increased pollutant
         discharges into recreation waterways.

1995   **The Clavey River Preservation Coalition**
         (California)
         Project: To seek Wild and Scenic protection for
         the Clavey River, Tuolumne County's only free-
         flowing river and a popular source of outdoor
         recreation.

| 1995 | **The Greater Ecosystem Alliance** (Washington) |
| | *Project:* To launch a public education campaign to bring protection for the North Cascades Ecosystem. |

| 1995 | **Canadian Parks and Wilderness Society** (Ontario) |
| | *Project:* To help protect the natural and recreational values of British Columbia's Northern Rockies ecosystem. |

| 1995 | **The American Mountain Foundation** (Colorado) |
| | *Project:* A two-year study to mitigate the impact of recreational usage in the alpine wilderness of Southeastern Colorado's Sangre de Cristo Range. |

| 1995 | **Northern Forest Alliance** (Vermont) |
| | *Project:* To introduce and pass a federal Northern Forest bill to protect the Northeast's critical wildlands. |

| 1995 | **Southwest Center for Biological Diversity** (New Mexico) |
| | *Project:* To fund a three-year direct citizen action campaign to help protect the San Pedro, the Southwest's last free-flowing river. |

| 1995 | **Utah Wilderness Coalition** (Utah) |
| | *Project:* To help launch a grassroots campaign to protect Utah's wild places. |

| 1996 | **Oregon Natural Desert Association** (Oregon) |
| | *Project:* To pursue the Oregon Clean Stream Campaign. |

| 1996 | **The Northern Alaska Environmental Center** (Alaska) |
| | *Project:* To strengthen citizen lobbying efforts through the Arctic Defense Lobby project. |

| 1996 | **Project Key West, Inc./d.b.a. Last Stand** (Florida) |
| | *Project:* Supports the Key West Saltponds Initiative, a comprehensive effort to restore and protect this sensitive region. |

| 1996 | **RESTORE: The North Woods** (Maine) |
| | *Project:* For activities to inform, organize and activate public support for a national park study of the Maine North Woods. |

| 1996 | **Headwaters Forest Coordinating Committee** (California) |
| | *Project:* To support the organization's efforts to mobilize public support and lobby Congress to secure permanent protection for Northern California's Headwaters Forest. |

| 1996 | **Trustees for Alaska** (Alaska) |
| | *Project:* Backs efforts to organize citizen participation to protect the Gulf of Alaska/Lower Cook Inlet marine region, which faces pressure from offshore development, and to raise national awareness of the area. |

| 1996 | **Friends of the River** (California) |
| | *Project:* To build public and legislative opposition to California's Auburn Dam, and support efforts to secure long-term protection for the North and Middle forks of the American River. |

1996   **Puget Soundkeeper Alliance** (Washington)
        Project: To support recreational users in launch-
        ing a "block watch" program for Washington's
        Puget Sound. The project includes recreation
        user stewardship, including public education and
        training to help detect sources of pollution in
        Puget Sound.

1996   **Lillian Anne Rowe Audubon Sanctuary**
        (Nevada)
        Project: Funds the formation of "Voices for the
        Platte," a coalition of people interested in pro-
        tecting the environmental and recreational
        values of the Platte River system.

1996   **The Access Fund** (Colorado)
        Project: Funds the purchase of an esssential ease-
        ment along Tennessee's Fiery Gizzard Trail to
        allow climbers access to the Foster Falls climb-
        ing area, and to complete trail improvements for
        key sections of the trail.

1997   **American Whitewater Affiliation** (Maryland)
        Project: To fund a campaign to protect and
        restore California's rivers through the relicens-
        ing of hydropower dams.

1997   **Canadian Parks & Wilderness Society**
        (Ontario)
        Project: Funds the Bow Valley Corridor Project
        protecting the migratory pathways for large car-
        nivores in the valley.

1997   **People for Puget Sound** (Washington)
        Project: To continue and expand a grassroots
        campaign to establish the Northwest Straits
        National Marine Sanctuary.

| 1997 | **Rivers Canada** (Quebec) |
| | *Project:* To support a coalition building effort on behalf of the preservation of the Taku watershed. |

| 1997 | **The Nature Conservancy of Utah** (Utah) |
| | *Project:* To assist with the purchase of the Dugout Ranch in southeastern Utah, protecting it from sale and subsequent development. |

| 1997 | **The Upper Chattahoochee Riverkeeper Fund** (Georgia) |
| | *Project:* To advocate the restoration, enhancement and protection of water and recreation resources in the Apalachicola-Chattahoochee-Flint and Alabama-Coosa-Tallapoosa river basins. |

| 1997 | **The John Muir Project** (California) |
| | *Project:* To improve recreation opportunities and redirect timber subsidies into worker retraining and ecological restoration by ending timber sales on federal land. |

| 1998 | **The Wild Utah Forest Campaign** (Utah) |
| | *Project:* To build support from key interest groups and the public for protection of wildlife habitat and recreational resources in Utah's remaining forest wild lands. |

| 1998 | **The Alliance for the Wild Rockies** (Montana) |
| | *Project:* To help gain support for the Northern Rockies Ecosystem Protection Act, H.R. 1425, a bill that represents the overall blueprint the grassroots conservation movement has for its vision of ecosystem protection in the northern Rockies. |

1998   **South Yuba River Citizens League**
(California)
Project: To help the citizen-based educational
organization with its efforts to protect dozens of
threatened and endangered species, as well as
recreation at the Yuba River watershed near
Marysville, California.

1998   **The River Network** (Oregon)
Project: For the purchase of Alberton Gorge to
protect it as a whitewater and recreational
resource. This segment of the Clark Fork River
in western Montana has recreational, scenic,
and historical values, and is threatened with
development.

1998   **Protect Kohanaiki 'Ohana** (Hawaii)
Project: To protect Hawaii's Kohanaiki coastline
from the impacts of development and ensure
that it is available for recreational use.
Accessible by jeep trails only, Kohanaiki is home
to one of the last remaining and most significant
wetland areas in Hawaii.

1998   **Friends of the River** (California)
Project: To provide permanent protection for key
rivers in California which are directly threatened
by new dam proposals.

1998   **Predator Project** (Montana)
Project: To both increase the public's awareness
of the prairie dog ecosystem in the northern
Plains region and get the public actively
involved in the future management and restoration of this imperiled escosystem.

1998   **Southwest Center for Biological Diversity**
            (Arizona)
            Project: To restore the health of the Colorado
            River Delta in Mexico.

1998   **Boulder-White Clouds Council** (Idaho)
            Project: To persuade the Forest Service managers
            of the Sawtooth Forest in Idaho to manage its
            own recommended Wilderness area as
            Wilderness and to improve its management of
            livestock grazing, mining and recreation.

1999   **Hells Canyon Preservation Council** (Oregon)
            Project: To defeat the Snake Wild and Scenic River
            motorization and wilderness de-classification bill
            in the 106th Congress.

1999   **Sea Turtle Restoration Project** (California)
            Project: To protect endangered sea turtles in
            ways that make cultural and economic sense to
            the communities that share the beaches and
            waters with these gentle creatures.

1999   **Southern Utah Wilderness Alliance** (Utah)
            Project: To ultimately protect as wilderness at
            least six million acres of Utah's unique redrock
            country under the 1964 Wilderness Act.

1999   **Grand Canyon Wildlands Council** (Arizona)
            Project: To protect and restore the remarkable
            array of native species and ecosystems in the vast
            lands linked to the Grand Canyon of the
            Colorado River.

1999   **Oregon Natural Resources Council** (Oregon)
            Project: To generate greater public involvement

for forest protection in Oregon; to provide greater clout within the forest-protection movement and stronger commitments from local government officials for forest protection in the state of Oregon.

1999   **The Wildlands Project** (Arizona)
Project: To fund a grassroots effort aimed at building public support for the restoration of North American wildlands.

1999   **Vahalla Wilderness Society** (British Columbia)
Project: For a media campaign aimed at building support for a 300,000-acre Spirit Bear Conservancy along the British Columbia coast. The region is a popular destination for hikers, backpackers and naturalists, and home to a rare white subspecies of black bear called Kermode or Spirit Bear.

1999   **South Yuba River Citizen's League** (California)
Project: For a campaign to permanently protect Northern California's South Yuba river by adding it to the state's Wild and Scenic River System.

1999   **Siskiyou Regional Education Project** (Oregon)
Project: To protect public lands surrounding the Siskiyou Rivers region in southwest Oregon, home to the highest concentration of wild rivers in the lower forty-eight states.

1999   **Ancient Forest International** (California)
Project: For its work to facilitate cooperation between private landowners and public agencies

to create a habitat-friendly open space for migratory fish and animals.

2000   **BC Spaces for Nature** (British Columbia)
        Project: To work toward extended permanent Wilderness protection in southwestern British Columbia's 7.5 million-acre Chilcotin Ark.

2000   **Utah Rivers Council** (Utah)
        Project: To fund the Bear River Coalition's efforts to protect this river and ecosystem for paddlers, hikers, and many other users through grassroots organization, educating and reforming the water district and lobbying the state legislature.

2000   **Save Our Wild Salmon** (Washington)
        Project: To provide resources for the Columbia and Snake Rivers Campaign to restore populations of wild salmon through partial removal of four federal dams on the Lower Snake River.

2000   **California Wilderness Coalition** (California)
        Project: To fund the CWC's Wildlands 2000 campaign to obtain Wilderness designation on California's remaining unprotected wilderness through coordinated public education, local outreach and lobbying efforts.

2000   **Oregon Natural Desert Association** (Oregon)
        Project: For the Steens Mountain Campaign proposing extension of Wilderness designation to this entire mountain located in the high desert of southeastern Oregon.

2000   **Southern Utah Wilderness Alliance** (Utah)
        Project: To protect as wilderness approximately nine million acres of Utah's unique redrock and

basin and range lands under the 1964
Wilderness Act.

2000   **Raincoast Conservation Foundation** (British
Columbia)
Project: To protect the mainland coast of British
Columbia known as the Great Bear Rainforest.
It contains the largest contiguous network of
low elevation, intact ancient temperate rainforest
left on the planet.

2000   **Pacific Crest Biodiversity Project**
(Washington)
Project: To support their effort to end old growth
logging in the national forests of the Pacific
Northwest.

2000   **Oregon Natural Resources Council** (Oregon)
Project: To support their effort to preserve nearly
5 million acres of wildlands in Oregon.

2000   **Appalachian Trail Conference** (West Virginia)
Project: To support their initiative to acquire and
protect portions of two of Maine's most spectacular mountains, Mount Abraham and
Saddleback Mountain.

Appendix iii

Conservation Alliance Members
As of January 2001

Adventure Photo & Film (Ventura, CA)

Altrec.com (Bellevue, WA)

American Alpine Institute, Ltd. (Bellingham, WA)

Atlas Snow-Shoe (San Francisco, CA)

Backpacker Magazine (Emmaus, PA)

Backpacker's Pantry, Inc. (Boulder, CO)

Belinda Sanda Sales (Redding, CA)

Blue Magazine (New York, NY)

Boulder Outdoor Survival School (Boulder, CO)

Burlington Industries (New York, NY)

Campmor, Inc. (Upper Saddle River, NJ)

Chaco Sandals (Paonia, CO)

Climbing Magazine (Carnondale, CO)

Columbia Sportswear (Portland, OR)

Eagle Creek Travel Gear (Vista, CA)

Eastern Mountain Sports, Inc. (EMS) (Peterborough, NH)

Edgeworks Inc. (Seattle, WA)

Flannel Design (Redmond, WA)

Galyan's Trading Company (Plainfield, IN)

Gear.com (Seattle, WA)

Grabber Performance Group (Fort Bragg, CA)

Grand Union Trading Co., Ltd. (Kowloon Bay, Hong Kong)

Gregory Mountain Products (Temecula, CA)

Hooked on the Outdoors (Dunwoody, GA)

Kelty Pack, Inc. (Boulder, CO)

Kennan Ward Photography (Santa Cruz, CA)

Kirwin Communications (Park City, UT)

Kokatat (Arcata, CA)

L.L. Bean (Freeport, ME)

Lotus Designs, Inc. (Weaverville, NC)

Lowe Alpine Systems (Broomfield, CO)

Lowepro Camera Bags (Markham, Ontario)

Marmot (Santa Rosa, CA)

Merrell Footwear (Rockford, MI)

Milliken and Co. (Spartanburg, SC)

Montrail (Seattle, WA)

Moonstone Mountain Equipment (Mercer Island, WA)

Mountain Equipment Co-op (Vancouver, British Columbia)

Mountain Hardwear, Inc. (Berkeley, CA)

National Geographic Adventure (New York, NY)

New Leaf Paper (San Francisco, CA)

Nike (Beaverton, OR)

The North Face (San Leandro, CA)

Outdoor Retailer (Laguna Beach, CA)

Outside Magazine (Santa Fe, NM)

Paddler Magazine (Springfield, VA)

Patagonia, Inc. (Ventura, CA)

Pearl Izumi (Broomfield, CO)

Perception, Inc. (Easley, SC)

Phoenix Creative (St. Louis, MO)

Planetoutdoors.com (Boulder, CO)

Polo Sport RLX (New York, NY)

Recreational Equipment, Inc. (REI) (Kent, WA)

Rennie Publications, Inc. (Collingwood, Ontario)

Riverside Design (Anacortes, WA)

Royal Robbins (Modesto, CA)

Sierra Designs (Emeryville, CA)

Sorensen's Resort (Hope Valley, CA)

Southern Exposure (Safety Harbor, FL)

Sporting Goods Manufacturers Association (North Palm Beach, FL)

Tesser.com (Boulder, CO)

Thor-Lo Sock Company (Statesville, NC)

The Timberland Company (Stratham, NH)

Trails Illustrated/National Geographic Maps (Evergreen, CO)

Vasque Division (Red Wing, MN)

Watergirl (Ventura, CA)

W.L. Gore & Associates, Inc. (Elkton, MD)

Index

Center for Marine Conservation, 122

Chain, David "Gypsy," 203

Cherney, Darryl, 192–93, 200, 205–6

Chilkat Eagle Preserve, 49

Chouinard, Yvon, xiv–xv, 11

Clark Fork River, Montana, 209–20

Clark, Mike, 135–36, 143–45

Clarks Fork, 129, 132

Clavey Falls, 151

Clavey River, 149–63

Clavey River Preservation Coalition (CRPC), 154, 157–62

Clean Water Act, 134

Clinton, Bill (U.S. President)/ Clinton administration, 31, 141–44, 198–202

Clune, Russ, 67

Coalition to Restore the Eastern Wolf (CREW), 180–81

Conservation Alliance, see Outdoor Industry Conservation Alliance

Cooke City, Montana, 127–45

Cowles, Macon, 195

Crockett, Kate, 199–200

Crown Land, 42

Crowne Butte Mines, 130–31

D

Dabney, Walt, 22

Dalton Post, 44

Daly, Joe, 157

Davidson, Sam, 71–72

Davis, Gray (California governor), 104

Dayton, Peter, 209–20

De Boer, Kristin, 176, 180–81

Defenders of Wildlife, 168

Department of Inland Fisheries and Wildlife, Maine, 178

Devlin, Sherry, 218

Doroff, Sue, 217

Dugout Ranch, Utah, 19–37

Duke of Abruzzi, 44

Dunn, Michael, 52

Dunning, Joan, 195

E

1872 Mining Law, 127, 132–34

Earth First!, 122, 192–93, 197–200, 202–4

Economic Enhancement Roundtable, 99–100

Edwards, Anne (Canadian minister of mining), 56

Edwards, Glenda, 160–62

Ellis, Libby, 33, 36, 70–71

W

Ward, Chip, 28
Warren, Seth, 211–12
Wasson, John, 13
Water Shed, The, 161
Watts, John, 4–5
Western Energy, 209
Wheatley, Beth, 182–83
Wiessner, Fritz, 59–62, 73
Wild and Scenic Rivers Act/
 status, 94, 95, 97, 98, 100,
 132, 151, 154, 156–57,
 159–63, 220
Wilderness Act, The, 29
Wilderness Society, The, 29,
 50, 104, 167
Williams, Mina, 117–18
Williams, Ted, 176–77, 179
Williams, Terry Tempest, 75,
 182
Wilson, Wendy, 1–17
Windy Craggy Mine/mountain,
 41–57
"Wise Use" movement, 97–99,
 179
Wolfe, Art, 52
Wood, JoAn, 14

Working Assets, 104
World Heritage Convention,
 49
World Heritage Sites, 49, 56
World Trade Organization, 122
World Wildlife Fund, 50
Wrangell–St. Elias National
 Park, 43
Wyoming Woolens, 137–38

Y

Yellowstone National
 Park/Greater Yellowstone
 ecosystem 22, 129, 132,
 136–37
Yellowstone River, Montana,
 127, 132
Yosemite National
 Park/Greater Yosemite,
 149–53, 161
Yuba County Water Agency,
 95, 101
Yule, Ralph, 212–13

Z

Zackheim, Hugh, 216–18
Zilligen, Jil, 136

About the Author

Formerly a nationally ranked competitive rock climber and ski guide, wilderness advocate and freelance writer Amy Irvine makes her home among the red rock canyons of southern Utah. Her work has appeared in *Climbing* and *Rock and Ice,* as well as in several anthologies of short stories.

The author and publisher gratefully acknowledge the following sources for permission to use copyrighted material and for their cooperation in fair use and public domain applications.

Canaries on the Rim: Living Downwind in the West by Chip Ward. Reprinted by permission of Verso publishers.

"gothic" from *Webster's Third New International® Dictionary, Unabridged*, copyright © 1993 Merriam-Webster, Incorporated.

Round River by Aldo Leopold, copyright © Oxford University Press. Reprinted by permission.

"What Happened Here Before" from *Turtle Island*, copyright © 1974 Gary Snyder. Reprinted by permission of New Directions Publishing Corp.